MUMPRENEUR
EVOLUTION

MUMPRENEUR EVOLUTION

On our terms

Edited by
Erin Thomas Wong

The Mumpreneur
COLLECTIVE

Contents

For all of you out there carving your own path

Introduction

Female entrepreneurs with children said that primary care responsibilities are the #1 barrier to further business success.
Rose Review of Female Entrepreneurship, HM Treasury 2019

A mumpreneur is a female entrepreneur who combines running a business with looking after her children. The word has caused some controversy, but I and many others find it the perfect term to describe how we have chosen to live our lives.

We have made a conscious decision not to replace a 60 hour a week corporate job with a 60 hour a week business, but instead to create flexible businesses which allow us to also be the primary carer for our children.

A business on our terms.

This book is for you if you are a mum running a business, or thinking of starting one, and want to hear from women who have learned the lessons so you don't have to.

My story

The moment that things changed for me was when I became pregnant, aged 29, with my first child. I had worked tirelessly to build my career in TV production, a job which I thrived on, but as a Production Manager in London I was working long hours, and at the beck and call of the crew. Although I loved it, as a lifestyle it was all consuming.

It slowly dawned on me that returning to work would mean putting our son in full-time childcare, which due to the high cost, would in turn reduce my contribution to the family income to just a few hundred pounds a month, and this was on a good salary!

Plus, as he got older, with the hours I was working I would never be able to pick him up from the school gates...

Was this really the kind of life that I had worked so hard to achieve?

I desperately wanted a successful and satisfying career. But I also wanted to be present for my child and not have to rely on wrap around childcare.

And here's what I know to be true: I am not the only one who feels this way.

With the ever increasing cost of childcare plus the inflexibility of many work cultures, when women want to return to work after having children we are often faced with a tough decision. It's an either/or: choose conventional employment or choose staying at home with their kids.

I strongly believe that we shouldn't have to make that choice, especially when there are alternatives.

That is why I decided to carve my own path and become a mumpreneur. I have chosen to run a business I love, make good money, and still have the flexibility to pick my kids up at the school gates. This way, I can be both a mother and a business owner side by side.

Mumpreneurship is the future

Mumpreneurs should not be underestimated. Figures show that, collectively, they are driving the UK's economic growth. According to a report published by Think Tank Development Economics, these power women generated £7.2 billion in revenue for the nation in 2014 and supported over 200,000 jobs. By 2025, the mumpreneur economy will generate £9.5 billion for the UK and add even more employees to their books.

Now, with the hugely disruptive economic impact of Covid-19, I believe we can expect to see a steep rise in the number of women exploring this path. Many families will re-assess their expectations of income, and many may also be prompted to rethink their values and lifestyles.

Most of these interviews took place before the onset of Covid-19. As this book goes to press in June 2020, we find ourselves in the position of being forced to re-evaluate, re-strategize and evolve our businesses to adapt to a new and, as yet unknown, future. We have no doubt, however, that we will rise to the challenge.

For more than a decade I have been supporting women in making the transition from mum to mumpreneur, and have been helping them to grow businesses which work for them around family life.

Back in 2016 I took this online, and launched The Mumpreneur Collective (then known as Making Mumpreneurs) – a free community where business women from around the world gather for advice, support and conversation. Together, they inspire and motivate each other to confront daily challenges and celebrate their successes.

The women featured in this book are all members of The Cocoon Business Club, the membership group within the Mumpreneur Collective which embraces women at various stages of their entrepreneurial journeys and offers high level training and expert support.

You'll meet professional high-fliers who gave up corporate careers to create and grow flexible businesses, women who realised there was a gap in the market which they could fill, plus women who are building businesses whilst solo-parenting and home schooling.

You'll meet women who started their businesses with babies in their arms, and are now exceeding their previous salaries; women who have chosen to work part-time around their children, and others who have created successful franchises and employment opportunities for other women at home.

This book offers snapshots of the lives of 23 mumpreneurs – what motivates them, what drives them on, and how they deal with difficult business challenges.

I want you to feel empowered and inspired by reading their

stories. I want you to learn from their mistakes and realise that you're not alone in the challenges you may be facing.

You will be encouraged by their tales of overcoming self-doubt, carving their own paths and winning their battles with fear of failure.

You will gain invaluable insights into how they made the transition from employment to starting a business, whether they have any regrets, how they have overcome imposter syndrome and how they measure success.

It's my hope that you'll see how possible this can be for you too. How you can overcome your own self-doubt, how you can carve your own path, and how you too can become a happy and successful business owner.

Want to learn how to survive and thrive as a mum in business? Read on!

How to get the most from this book

1. Use the 'key takeaway' section at the end of each story to write down what resonated with you, and any lightbulb moments their story has sparked.

2. At the back of the book you'll find out where to download your free Mumpreneur Evolution workbook to help you collate all of your thoughts, so that you can take action and start making a difference in your own business straight away.

ZOE KEEPING

Business Name: Rock the Bump
pregnant belly casting
Website: www.rockthebumpbellycasting.co.uk

Rock the Bump founder & belly cast artist, Zoe
Keeping is a mumpreneur and small business owner
with a passion for supporting other women. Rock
the Bump is a bespoke pregnant belly casting studio
based in Bournemouth, Dorset founded in March
2015. Zoe works with women from across the UK to
celebrate their beautiful bumps and create timeless,
unique pregnancy keepsake casts. Zoe's celebrity
clients include Myleene Klass and Cara De La Hoyde.

What did you do for a living before having children?
Before having children, work was my everything. I was in full-
time employment working as a Senior Adviser for the national
homelessness charity, Shelter. I was the main bread-winner
with a good salary, great benefits and a pension. I worked long
hours in a stressful environment, with targets to meet and
people's homes and lives at stake.

**Why did you decide to have a career change after
becoming a mum?**
I started my own business back in March 2015 whilst on
maternity leave with my second child. I wanted to do
something for myself that I enjoyed, offer more flexibility and
provide a better fit around family life. I had worked for other
people for 22 years, starting with South Herefordshire District
Council when I was 19, then The Children's Society when I
moved to Bournemouth in 1997, followed by 12 years with

Shelter and a stint with the national parenting charity NCT. Then, in February 2017 and on maternity leave with my third child, I took a leap of faith and made the decision to leave my 'day job' in order to concentrate on building my business and looking after my young family. It was when I got the routine call from my boss checking in to discuss my return to work that, without thinking, amidst the chaos of my life with three happy little hooligans, I made a BIG decision and responded by telling her that I would not be coming back to work at the end of my maternity leave. Yep, I quit my job to follow my dreams, look after my family and build my business.

Did you struggle to make the transition to business owner?

Self-employment is a funny old thing, especially when your business is an artistic one. Being a self-employed artist and a work-at-home mum to three children is especially funny, firstly because everyone assumes that you don't have a job, and secondly because you have to fit your work in to any little slither of time you might be able to find if you want to make a go of it. The fact that it took some time to start generating a profit from the business definitely contributed to my self-doubt. Looking back, I was almost embarrassed to tell people that I had my own business because I knew that their response would be to ask how much money I was making. I felt like a bit of a fraud if I'm honest and was often racked with guilt, thinking that I had selfishly put my family under financial pressure in order to make a go of my own business.

At times I struggled to stay focused and keep my business

"The fact that it took some time to start generating a profit from the business definitely contributed to my self-doubt."

on track. I would waste valuable time and energy thinking about my competitors, get nervous and start looking at ways to expand Rock the Bump so I could make more money quickly even though it wasn't what I really wanted to do. I had to stay true to myself and continue to create beautiful pregnant belly bump casts and belly bowls that I was proud of. It took time to recognise the value of my own work and to be able to better sell myself.

Was there a lightbulb moment or a turning point where it all "clicked" for you?

A big turning point for me was when Love Island 2016 winner and The Only Way is Essex star Cara De La Hoyde tweeted "Can anyone recommend where to get a pregnancy body cast done? Something like this but decorated, thanks" on 17 September 2017. I couldn't help but get a little excited! I tweeted a reply and emailed Cara's agent. Everything moved very quickly from there on in and, just under a week later (on my birthday I should add!), Cara's Rock the Bump pregnant belly casting session was all booked in ahead of her 30 November due date. Cara took to Instagram and live streamed her Rock the Bump casting session with me which was picked up and featured in OK! Magazine online leading to a huge increase in followers for my business. The growth from just under 500 followers to 1.5K plus led to a notable increase in enquiries from pregnant women across the UK who want a Rock the Bump pregnant belly casting. The significant thing here is the growth of my brand as I am now seeing more women who specifically want me to create their pregnancy keepsake cast and are willing to travel and pay to make it happen.

I went on to be shortlisted as a finalist in the MPower National Business Awards 2018 where I was highly commended in the 'Self-Belief' category and Jacqueline Gold CBE acknowledged me as one of her WOW Winners on Twitter.

"It took time to recognise the value of my own work and to be able to better sell myself."

In 2019 I had the pleasure of working with the fabulous Myleene Klass, creating a beautiful Rock the Bump pregnant belly casting for her. Images of the casting session that took place at Myleene's home attracted huge media interest and were featured in national press, magazines and widely shared across social media.

Subsequently, I was invited to The Sun newspaper office in London to create a Rock the Bump pregnant belly cast for a lovely mum-to-be as part of what turned out to be a full-page feature 'I've had plaster Klasst of bump like Myleene'. Friends and family started to take notice of what I had achieved and acknowledge the hard work I had put in to get to this point. I felt validated and 100% more confident as a business owner.

What does success look like to you?
Success for me is more about recognition than money. Don't get me wrong, money is nice, and my mindset definitely changed when I started making a profit, but I genuinely love what I do, and it means so much to me when women choose me to create their bump cast.

How does your work/life balance look?
Whilst being a working Mum can often be a hindrance, in my field of work, it helps! Having to work around family commitments allows me to offer my clients flexibility that I wouldn't necessarily be able to do if I was working 9-5 hours. I often travel to see women on weekends, combining a bump casting booking with an impromptu day trip or short break.

"Remember that your closest friends are not necessarily your target audience so don't look to them for approval."

Zoe Keeping

I'm fortunate to have a husband who is very supportive of me and my business ventures and lucky to have children who love going on road trips, visiting new places and helping me grow my business.

My work/life balance is constantly evolving as the needs of my young family and my business change. Every day is different as I juggle to fit in my "bump work" (as my little ones call it!) alongside everything else. Weekends are when I get the most time to focus on Rock the Bump, often seeing clients for casting sessions on Saturdays and spending time in my home studio or garden on Sundays getting messy – strengthening and smoothing casts, painting, finishing and preparing casts ready for clients to hang/display in their homes. I rely heavily on social media to promote my business, search out new leads and potential collaborations, so I battle with the inevitable "mum guilt" daily as I'm constantly checking on my phone, but it's so worth it. I love the fact that I can be on the sofa breast-feeding a sleepy toddler and working at the same time. The opportunities that can arise from a simple comment, like or share on Twitter, Instagram and Facebook never cease to amaze me!

One of the things I love most about Rock the Bump is that my little people enjoy it and seem to quite like "mummy's bumps" all over the house. To them it's not really a job, they just see mum getting messy, painting, creating... the downside to this is that people can easily forget that Rock the Bump IS my job, my business, my livelihood and not just an expensive hobby!

What does a typical work day look like for you?

No two days are the same. My husband leaves the house for work before any of us are awake so my weekday mornings are frenetic to say the least! I try to grab a shower before the kids need to get ready for school. Then it's the onslaught of preparing breakfast and packed lunches for my three children.

My head's often spinning at this point as I'm also checking emails and responding to new enquiries and comments that have come through my various social media channels. At 8:30am I get to walk my two oldest children to school before dropping my three year old at the childminder's.

On my way home I stick in my headphones and find a podcast to listen to that will inspire me and help to get me in the right headspace for my working day. Once home I have roughly five hours before it's pick up time. I normally get straight to it, more coffee, podcast on loud speaker, log in to my emails and start responding to enquiries and planning in castings in my diary.

Once I'm up to date on admin I'll get to work on sanding, smoothing and painting belly casts. I'll take breaks now and again to do little jobs around the house that need to be done and, where possible, I'll try and dedicate some time to working on content for my website and social media.

In the blink of an eye it's time to pick up the kids. We'll catch up on each other's days, maybe head to the park for a bit of a play and some much needed fresh air before heading home. I love being able to do school pick ups and only miss them on the days when I'm out of town for a belly casting session (in which case my husband will juggle his work to finish early so he can do pick up). My husband is normally home soon after and we work together to sort out dinner, homework, bathtimes, bedtimes before crashing in front of the TV at around 9pm.

"A coping strategy that has helped me is to communicate with my husband, so he is fully aware of any work deadlines or pressure I am under."

I'll still find myself looking at my phone and picking up emails, messages etc throughout the evening as that's often the time that my customers are active on social media and wanting to find out more about Rock the Bump. I am getting better at switching off now and will often head up to bed with a good book, leaving my phone safely tucked away in my office until the morning when it all starts over again!

How important has it been to have the right support and what impact has having that support had on your business and success?

I could have thrown in the towel more times than I care to remember but I've always held on to the belief that I could, and would, eventually build a successful business doing something I genuinely LOVE and being a full-time mum to my three young children.

As a working mum I often feel very isolated. I struggle to get to any face-to-face networking meetings and any 'spare' time I do have available is spent working. I joined 'The Cocoon', an online networking club that offers me the chance to network and access support as well as helping me to feel like I'm a part of something bigger. It is really empowering and has helped spur me on to grow my businesses and take chances I might not have previously thought possible.

A coping strategy that has helped me is to communicate with my husband, so he is fully aware of any work deadlines or pressure I am under. This is vital because everything I do is at home and it's easy for boundaries to get blurred. I am fortunate to now have my own work space which means I have a place to go to when I need to focus. Making sure that my family understands when I have an important piece of work to finish, or an important phone call to make, helps ease some of the pressure. Another coping strategy is to know when to STOP! I am slowly learning that it's sometimes better to just stop work when the children are causing mayhem and give them the time they need. Then, once they are happy and I feel less stressed, I can return to my own work and focus better.

If you had your time again, is there anything you would do differently?

Be less modest about my achievements! I can't help but wonder how different things would have been for me in terms of business growth if I had the confidence to shout it from the roof-tops and really sell myself in the early days rather than waiting for opportunities to come my way.

What's next for you?

I'm looking forward to working with many more women to create custom, artistic pregnant belly bump & belly bowl keepsake casts and offering a bespoke mentoring package for other artists wishing to learn the art of belly-casting. In terms of business growth, my aim is to invest in my website and social media marketing strategy to help reach an even wider audience and make a Rock the Bump belly cast a 'must have' item for all mums to be! I would like to see Rock the Bump pregnant belly casting at The Baby Show and am hopeful for more lucrative celebrity collaborations and endorsements.

Zoe's Top Tips:

1. Surround yourself with other passionate, motivated, entrepreneurial women.

2. Remember that your closest friends are not necessarily your target audience so don't look to them for approval.

3. Be creative, work hard and do something special.

Key Takeaway

_____

_____

_____

_____

_____

_____

_____

_____

_____

_____

ANNE MILLNE-RILEY

Business Name: Confidence Guru
Website: www.confidenceguru.com

Anne Millne-Riley is a Confidence
Coach, Trainer and founder of
Confidence Guru. She works with
clients who are struggling with their self-belief
to help them to overcome obstacles and develop
their self-confidence. Anne originally qualified as a
Psychotherapist but began to develop a passion for
empowering others and recently published her first
book 'Confidence Guru – Discover a Confident You!'

What did you do for a living before having children?
Before starting my business eight years ago, I worked in the
advertising industry for many years as a Media Buyer, and then
as an Education Officer for my local council – it was actually
my job to persuade the general public to cease littering! This
meant organising community litter picks, creating anti-litter
campaigns and talking to anyone on TV and radio who would
listen. The role pushed me outside my comfort zone at times
but it helped me to be self-motivated and I had to become
more innovative and creative. This experience gave me many
of the skills I have used in setting up my own business.

**Why did you decide to have a career change after
becoming a mum?**
Becoming a mother has been the most exciting and rewarding
thing I have ever done with my life. A few years later I became
a single mum and had to find ways of earning a living whilst
being there for my children. I was determined to find a career

that fitted around family responsibilities and that is when my first business, and then later Confidence Guru, were founded. Being able to work during school hours but still be at the school gates to collect them each day, and to spend time with my boys was the driving force behind the change.

Did you struggle to make the transition to business owner?

Going it alone was scary at first but I knew I had to make it work. I had already tried paid employment but I always ended up feeling guilty that I wasn't spending enough time with my boys.

There were some low points at the beginning. I remember selling my old business suits and books at a car boot sale in order to fund my website! And, one week, three clients had booked appointments but only one of them turned up. However, I genuinely believe that if you work hard and really believe in your business it will succeed! I will never forget my first paying customer – I felt elated and soon began to enjoy seeing each client make progress as we worked together.

One of the biggest considerations in building my business was money! Childcare is so expensive and I did not have any family to help out with babysitting so when I began, it was all about keeping a small employed income which ran alongside my self-employed work. Having the flexibility around time with the children has been wonderful. I didn't earn a great deal of money originally but I now earn three times as much as I did when I was employed. I must have been a good role model, as

"There were some low points at the beginning. I remember selling my old business suits and books at a car boot sale in order to fund my website!"

"Don't give up ... everyone started out at the beginning just like you!"

Anne Millne-Riley

my 23 year old son set up his own business three months ago and I am happy to have been able to support him in this.

Was there a lightbulb moment or a turning point where it all "clicked" for you?

At the beginning, I saw clients in a room at the front of my home. Although I did my best to make this look professional, it didn't give the impression I was hoping for. But as my client numbers grew it became necessary to find myself an office. Up until this point I had felt like I was "trying to start" a business, but when I found an office, moved in my desk and some nice pot plants, it felt like I had stepped up a gear! As I erected large window signs featuring my logo I realized I really had created a fully formed business of my own. Having an office had been a goal, and achieving it made me more confident and finally enabled me to create the impression I wanted to make on my clients.

What does success look like to you?

For me, success means free time with my now husband and family. I am aware that the more successful my business becomes the closer I get to achieving the right mix. Publishing my first book and beginning to receive a small income from it felt like a significant step forward but I still have some way to go in realizing my business and life ambitions. However, helping my son recently with an assignment and being able to really give him my full attention is something I couldn't have done had I been working for someone else and makes me realise I am succeeding!

How does your work/life balance look?

I have to admit that when you are building a business this can be one of your biggest challenges. Some weeks I work long hours and do what I have to do to keep driving the business forward, but working for myself now means I am always there to share important family events and occasions. I am now able to go to the gym or attend my salsa class. As the business develops further I hope to spend more of my time on leisure pursuits.

What does a typical work day look like for you?
Ahh, my days can vary but here goes...

Up at 7am, make myself look smart (in a very short space of time – I am a mum after all – we are resourceful!)

At 8am I prepare sessions for that day's clients and send any emails that need to be answered before the start of the day. At 9am I might be seeing the first of my clients, helping them to identify their limiting beliefs, exploring their strengths and working on strategies to help them to get to the next stage in their business, career or personal goals.

Lunchtime, I often have a hasty lunch, sometimes with my (now 24 year old) son who has recently launched his first business, sharing news and exchanging advice – him helping me with something social media related and me helping him to compile an email to a new customer. It's lovely collaborating with your children.

In the afternoon, I may have a few more client sessions and perhaps speak at a 'ladies in business' network meeting before returning home for tea kindly prepared by my husband.

Throughout the day I am responding to emails and text enquiries, sometimes from my younger son who is in his first year of university...' How do you cook chicken?', 'Can you give me some feedback on my essay if I send it to you?', or 'Can I borrow some money?'. I might hoover or take the duster for a spin around other tasks… I'm always on the go. I often finish work around 7pm… but I am working on finishing earlier!

My days are busy but I usually enjoy them.

How important has it been to have the right support and what impact has having that support had on your business and success?

Starting your own business can be a lonely affair! Having support and encouragement from others is vital in helping you to succeed. Being able to communicate with others in The Cocoon and developing my skills and knowledge through the masterclasses has definitely helped fill in the knowledge gaps and boosted my confidence. My biggest support has been my husband who has helped me to prepare for presentations and workshops, and my kids who both told me they were proud of me when I published my book!

If you had your time again, is there anything you would do differently?

I would definitely have started my own business many years before!! I love the challenge of building a business and ultimately being the architect of my own destiny. I never get the 'Sunday evening feeling' before work on the Monday and genuinely enjoy what I do. Being able to help others to find their voice is the most rewarding part of my role, and my client's appreciation for helping them to change their lives is lovely to receive.

What's next for you?

I am busy developing my training courses and workshops and hope to do more of this type of work over the coming years. Since publishing the book I have been asked to speak at more events and I am enjoying that too!

Anne's Top Tips:

1. Connect with other mumpreneurs for support, information and inspiration.

2. Don't give up – everyone started out at the beginning just like you.

3. Realise that being a mother has taught you amazing skills, patience, perseverance, multi-tasking and the art of persuasion.

Key Takeaway

_____

_____

_____

_____

_____

_____

_____

_____

_____

KERI SQUIBB

Business Name: 'The Dog and I' and
'The Soap Coach'
Website: www.thedogandi.co.uk and
www.thesoapcoach.co.uk

Keri Squibb has spent her entire working life
employed by others and still is. In the last five years,
alongside this, she has retrained as a dog groomer;
developed a successful brand of luxury handmade
dog grooming products, and begun teaching soap-
making. She is mum to two boys and stepmum to a
boy and a girl. She has a long suffering husband and
a houseful of animals.

What did you do for a living before having children?
I worked in a bank for ten years and went on to join my local
police force. I had my children whilst in the police and went
back part-time. I am still a part-time police officer but with an
end date in sight for 2021.

**Why did you decide to have a career change after
becoming a mum?**
In my case my change of direction came about not entirely
because I became a mum. I wanted the ability to stay part-time
at my day job but also work from home flexibly and be there
for the boys when I needed to be. I had always wanted to work
with animals – a cliche I know – and one thing led to another,
and it became a business. I certainly did not foresee I would
end up teaching soapmaking as well!

As it happens I am now on my 2nd and 3rd business in the
last five years. All have enabled me to work flexibly from home

which has made school holidays more manageable. I would not say easier, but I hope the boys will look back and think I was here for them a lot of the time.

Did you struggle to make the transition to business owner?

My main struggles have been time and tech. I still dislike tech but I know it is necessary and without it I would have no online business. I am still struggling with time – it is a work in progress! In the early days I also struggled with confidence in myself. I used to feel terrified that customers would think my products were terrible, and every time I got an email or a Facebook message I would expect a complaint. But the positive feedback was incredible, I still get so many lovely messages about my soap in particular and I still never fail to be slightly surprised.

On the plus side I don't worry about getting complaints now, and if I ever do get one then I imagine I will deal with it and move on. I do feel the classic mother guilt that I always appear to my family to be working but I think it bothers me more than them if I am honest. I did ask my youngest last year if he felt I was always working and he said not really so I must be doing something right.

Was there a lightbulb moment or a turning point where it all "clicked" for you?

My lightbulb moment was coming up with my niche: Soap for Dogs. At first I think people possibly thought I was crazy,

"I do feel the classic mother guilt that I always appear to my family to be working but I think it bothers me more than them if I am honest."

> "Mother guilt is a real thing. Acknowledge it and move on. Just because you are a mum does not mean you cannot pursue your dreams..."

Keri Squibb

#MumpreneurEvolution

even though I was a little crazy and doubted myself but I stuck with it, I knew deep down it was a genius product, plastic free, natural, effective, economical and I believed in it.

When it was awarded Best Dog Skincare Product in 2018 for my dog soap – I thought to myself 'well I guess it must be ok then' I still have to remind myself that it is a damn good product and it deserves the credentials. Since then the business has gone from strength to strength.

What does success look like to you?

Success to me is the business growing and moving forward all the time, however slowly that may be. Always having goals to work towards, happy customers and a sense of achievement. Paying myself a reasonable wage is not, to me, being successful, that is a non negotiable, not a measure of success. If we are not paying ourselves a wage we have a hobby not a business.

Becoming a business owner has enabled me to go part-time in my day job and earn money more flexibly. It has also given me the confidence to take early retirement from the police force next year and go all out on my business. I am confident that my business has the potential to earn me far greater rewards than I would ever attain in employment.

How does your work/life balance look?

My work/life balance is quite disjointed at present due to my shift work. My constant days off are Mondays and Wednesdays and I will always spend the majority of those days either making products, doing admin or both. I shoehorn a lot of hours into spare pockets of time between household and family commitments.

I am often on my laptop at 7am for half an hour, then I get the boys up for school, take the dogs out then come back to do a couple of hours more work then go to my day job for an eight hours late shift. That is the challenge for me juggling the business(es) alongside my day job. I won't pretend it has been easy, there have been tears and overwhelm along the way but I have a goal in sight and that keeps me going plus I am utterly convinced it will be worth it.

What does a typical work day look like for you?

My working week on the business side of things is generally condensed into 2 days due to other commitments, so those days start early and finish late. My husband leaves for work at 7am so he brings me a cup of tea in bed and I will generally log on to the laptop and answer emails, and have a quick check through social media for 30 mins before getting up.

The boys are old enough to get themselves up for school now so after making sure they are awake and moving, I will print out any postage labels for orders in the last 24 hours and get those packaged up and I am ashamed to say breakfast is normally eaten while I am stood up printing labels!

By 8.30am everyone has left the house and gone to school and I am normally straight out of the door to take the dogs out - I take them out in the van usually to nearby fields and then do the post office drop on the way back. I have a quick whizz round with the hoover and I then tidy the kitchen, put any washing on etc, empty the dishwasher if it needs it and then I leave to go to my workshop where I can generally be found between about 10am and 4pm.

At the workshop I will either be making soap, cutting soap, planning workshops, clearing up from previous workshops, doing admin, the list goes on. I often take this time to listen to business related podcasts too.

The boys let themselves in after school but I like to be home by 4 if possible as I really do not like them coming home to an empty house. I then have a chat with them, sometimes go shopping, my husband is usually home by 4.30pm and we always eat together if we can. I then hide myself away for another hour or so of admin or planning before finally packing up any larger trade orders that may be ready to go out, and then finally sitting down around 8.30 pm.

"The best few hundred pounds I have ever spent was on a course which quite literally baby-walked me through identifying my ideal client, things to include on my website, SEO, use of pop ups, and email funnels."

How important has it been to have the right support and what impact has having that support had on your business and success?

Without support I would not be where I am today. There is a saying that runs along the lines of 'Behind every successful woman in business there are another ten behind her that have her back' That is so true and I remember it all the time.

My support network has been extensive and ranges from The Cocoon business club where I know I can always hop in and ask a question however small and I will get a good answer, to other small business owners in my niche who have been just incredible, they know who they are, and my husband has also been amazing. I know I have probably driven him insane over the last few years but he trusts my judgement and is always supportive of my decisions. I have also invested in online courses when I have needed help. I really do recommend this if you can find one that covers the help you need.

The best few hundred pounds I have ever spent was on a course which quite literally baby walked me through identifying my ideal client, things to include on my website, SEO, use of pop ups, and email funnels. I then booked a weekend away with the dog and worked my way through the 20 hours of video tutorials and implemented everything without interruptions. It was intense but it worked and saved me hours of research in the long run. I have also purchased a mindset course which was awesome – I have achieved more in the last four months since doing it than I expected to achieve in the next two years.

If you had your time again, is there anything you would do differently?

If I had my time again I would absolutely have become self-employed sooner! Whilst the police has given me a comfortable lifestyle it has not been my life's calling. I don't get the buzz I get from my business and I certainly don't get the control. I love being able to call the shots, make my own decisions, take a day off if I want to, take a risk if I need to. And the feeling of achievement.

In many ways running your own business is far harder than being employed. It does sometimes seem to be 24/7 and there is no sick pay but I never get bored and there are far more highs than I have ever had in my day job.

What's next for you?

My next step is to rent commercial premises, a huge leap but I need to do this to grow my business. After that, who knows? What I have learned is that the business evolves and has taken me in directions I did not anticipate but which I have embraced.

For me at least, having a plan has not been a requirement – if I see an opportunity that interests me I will go for it, I am not suggesting we should go down a route that has no bearing on our business whatsoever but neither should we be blinkered to opportunity. In my case this has been recognising that there is a market for teaching soap-making as well as the retail side.

"What I have learned is that the business evolves and has taken me in directions I did not anticipate but which I have embraced."

Sometimes you will not spot an opportunity until much further down the line. For example, I would not have even considered the teaching aspect at the start of my business as I did not have the experience or credibility to pitch myself as an 'expert'. I don't like that word but if you have a skill, you are good at it and you are successful in creating a business from that skill then I guess it does mean you are well placed to share the knowledge and expertise, and add another string to your bow. None of us knows what is around the corner and flexibility is a real asset.

Keri's Top Tips:

1. Believe in yourself. You are never too old/inexperienced/busy to start something new.

2. Try not to expect your partner/spouse to understand anything about your business. And don't be offended if they are not that interested. This is your dream, not theirs.

3. Mother guilt is a real thing. Acknowledge it and move on. Just because you are a mum does not mean you cannot pursue your dreams – life does not stop for 20 years.

Key Takeaway

_____

_____

_____

_____

_____

_____

_____

KATHERINE WHITBY

Business Name: Baby Steps
Website: www.baby-steps.co.uk

Katherine is a Paediatric Nurse
and Health Visitor with 25 years
experience in the NHS. In 2006 she
established 'Baby Steps' offering Baby and Child
First Aid and Weaning courses in the comfort of
people's homes or at the Baby Steps Studio near
Guildford. Katherine supports new parents and babies
in their first steps together.

What did you do for a living before having children?
After leaving school I trained at Great Ormond Street Hospital
for Sick Children and worked there on qualifying before
moving to Paediatric A&E at Chelsea and Westminster in
London. After working shifts for years, I needed more of a
work/life balance. By this point I had met my future husband
and was not seeing much of him! I moved into the Community
and trained and worked as a Health Visitor. Strains on the
NHS were ever more evident with baby groups and parent
education classes being cut. I could see a real gap. Parents
wanted and needed information but were not receiving it.

In 2006 I started Baby Steps, offering First Aid courses
for parents in their homes and at local venues. I then added
Weaning and Baby Massage classes. I did this alongside full-
time Health Visiting and then dropped to four days a week to
give more time to Baby Steps. I was looking ahead to when I
hoped we would have a family, to build something which would
work around family life as well as something I enjoyed and
met a need.

Why did you decide to have a career change after becoming a mum?

The business had already been running for three years by the time I had my first child. Returning from maternity leave I changed my NHS job so it was local and only two days a week. I turned Baby Steps 'up or down' depending on how much time I could give to it, whilst juggling childcare and making it financially worthwhile when the children were small.

Did you struggle to make the transition to business owner?

I am a Nurse so have no business training at all! Nursepreneurs are rare and initially I felt almost like I was doing something that wasn't allowed. However, I knew many doctors, physiotherapists and other health professionals doing private work. I took advice from my governing body and union and went step by step. Working in the NHS I was, as someone pointed out to me, institutionalized, so being self-employed and starting a business was all very unknown. I was concerned about what my NHS colleagues would think and so didn't tell them for a while. There was a lot of tension in the workplace with burnout and stress, so I didn't want to add fuel to the fire. Even 14 years on, I still get imposter syndrome when things are quiet, and currently I am trying to establish myself in a new area which is tough. I come back to my experience and that this is a service parents need and would like and pick myself up again. Sometimes I feel pressure from people telling

"I am a Nurse so have no business training at all! Nursepreneurs are rare and initially I felt almost like I was doing something that wasn't allowed."

me I 'should' do something. However, I trust my instincts and experience in deciding what will work best for me, my business and with family life.

Was there a lightbulb moment or a turning point where it all "clicked" for you?

There have been many lightbulb moments in the last 14 years. Usually they have been because I have had feedback from parents about how the courses have helped them which makes my heart absolutely glow and makes it all worthwhile. I have feedback from professionals who have seen children in A&E whose parents have done my courses and tell me what they learnt really helped in an emergency situation or through a difficult time with feeding, or when struggling as a new parent. I keep a collection of stories and testimonies. Other lightbulb moments involve looking at the number of bookings Baby Steps has had in a month, year et cetera. It is so satisfying because it confirms it ia a viable business and clarifies I am offering a service parents want and need.

What does success look like to you?

I measure my success primarily in time. How much time do I have with my children? My family and friends? Am I at home during the school holidays? Evenings? Weekends? Do I have time to myself to be able to step back and take a deep breath? Also in job satisfaction, that is to say, the impact of my courses on new parents and their babies. Seeing parents' shoulders relax during courses as they feel less daunted, worried, anxious

"My aim is to give confidence and reassurance to parents every day and I really feel this happens. That is success! "

is incredible as I know that a happy parent = a happy baby. Having feedback that they were worried about weaning but now feel excited; that the choking technique saved their child's life; knowing I have given parents confidence to trust their instincts and believe in themselves, and the positive impact this has for the whole family. My aim is to give confidence and reassurance to parents every day and I really feel this happens. That is success! While the courses are First Aid and Weaning, many different issues arise such as maternal mental health or isolation. They are all part of the support I offer.

How does your work/life balance look?

Now both of the children are in full-time school my work is very much in school hours. This is very different to when they were small when I worked more evenings and weekends as it was easier to manage childcare when my husband was at home. I still run some courses in the evenings and at weekends but these are minimal as they impact on family life plus I then need childcare. I like that my children have seen me build my business. They help me prepare my materials, and I ask for their opinions and ideas. It is very much a family business and interwoven into our family life. They talk about it with pride. I feel it is a good example to them as I do something that I genuinely love, that helps people, and that I have created myself.

What does a typical work day look like for you?

So every week is different for me but this is actually one of the things I love about my job - the variety!

Typically I try to do a HITT workout first thing in the morning 4-5 days a week. I would have honestly laughed out loud at the thought of this a year ago, but I have felt so many benefits physically and mentally, I find it the best way to start the day.

I get myself and the kids ready and try to tidy, put washing

"She believed she could and she almost did but then someone asked her repeatedly for a snack until she forgot what she was doing so she didn't."

Social Mums

#MumpreneurEvolution

and dishwasher on before doing the school run. If I am working from home I will do any chores I need to before sitting down with my breakfast and laptop and do emails, calls and admin. Some days this lasts until school pickup, other days I will go to meetings, networking, run errands, do course prep or read.

If I am doing a Baby Steps course I will head off after drop off, either to London, the Coast or wherever it takes me! Or it may be in the Studio. I finish the course, often popping to the supermarket on the way and then get to school in time for pickup.

After school is clubs, homework, tea etc and I try not to be distracted by work which can be hard sometimes! After they have gone to bed some evenings if I am particularly fired up or need to do some course prep I will do some in the evenings, but I love having a hot bath, putting my pjs on and watching some TV, catching up with my husband who will now be home and getting into bed with my book. Cosy evenings all the way for me!

How important has it been to have the right support and what impact has having that support had on your business and success?

Looking back, I was very much on my own in the early years, with no nursing colleagues to seek advice or support from as it was very much a new venture. Later, other nurses came on board offering the courses with me. I have over the years built a valuable network which includes other nurses who also offer some private work, and fellow mums-in-business who understand running a business around family life.

Joining the online support of Erin's Cocoon has been incredible as it offers practical business advice to help Baby Steps grow but also a fantastic community who have my back. We recently moved from London where I had run Baby Steps for 13 years. Now I am endeavoring to build a new local network but appreciate this will take time which is hard! I continue to draw on advice and support from my established tribe.

I actually love working for myself, working on my own. The days fly by. However, it is vital to meet up with and to chat to my colleagues, as they have all become in their different ways. This includes the amazing Momentum Day held by The Mumpreneur Collective!

I take my professional accountability as a Nurse very seriously and have to 'revalidate' every three years to keep my registration by demonstrating I have completed enough hours of work, study and reflected on my practice. I love regularly attending courses and this ensures I deliver the most up-to-date information. I regularly do shifts in Paediatric A&E. I like wearing my uniform and working 'on the shop floor' but it also massively helps my credibility and parents love that I currently work there.

If you had your time again, is there anything you would do differently?

Honestly and quite unbelievably no! It has and continues to be a journey – highs and lows, success and experiences to learn from. If someone had told me years ago I would be a mum of two, running Baby Steps and doing shifts in A&E I would have been over the moon! It really is the dream for me. I never take it for granted. I am not aiming for a multi-million pound business. To earn enough money, doing something I love, that makes a positive difference – all those boxes are ticked. As a parent, I have always run the business to suit the different ages and stages of my children. So far Baby Steps has been able to evolve around that. I am so mindful the children are growing up so fast, so I am making the most of every moment.

What's next for you?

We made a big move away from London to Guildford in 2019. We are thrilled with the move for so many reasons but the hardest thing is Baby Steps has taken a real knock. Having had a successful business in London, I thought it would be transferable to our new area. While I am sure it is, it is taking longer than I thought to build up local business. The population is smaller here. I am establishing a new network, with a new website and ads. Word of mouth and my website continue to be the most effective ways to get business. It is frustrating but I really believe it will be a success here too. Just as it did 14 years ago, it will take time. We have an amazing studio at our new house, with parking. It is the perfect venue and works so incredibly well. I love doing home courses so I would like to do them locally. I also love the variety that comes with travelling to different places to teach my courses. So what is next is: to build my network here, establish my venue with regular bookings and have local home courses. I continue to travel back to London, which is great, but I have to manage this to make sure it isn't too much! The challenge currently is knowing what are the most effective ways of getting my name out there but not feeling overwhelmed.

Katherine's Top Tips:

1. Don't rush into it – you never get the time back with your children.

2. There is only one you – don't worry if other people are doing something similar, do it your way – people buy you.

3. Enjoy the journey – it is all part of your story – the challenges and the wonderful rewards.

Key Takeaway

_____

_____

_____

_____

_____

_____

_____

_____

_____

JO BRIANTI

Business Name: JLB Support
Solutions
Website: www.jlbsupportsolutions.co.uk

Jo Brianti is a Business Consultant who works with
service businesses to help them develop the right
systems/toolset, support configuration, deliver
training and where required provide ongoing
support. She has a passion for GDPR and helps small
businesses to implement best practices to support
compliance within their business.

What did you do for a living before having children?

Prior to having children I worked as a Project Analyst Manager
with a focus on working within a PMO framework. I worked
in large teams delivering IT/business transformation projects
for companies such as Jaguar Cars, TfL, TUI, MFI/Howdens
Joinery and the Medical Research Council. I had also
established a project management office for the IT department
of a national FTSE-listed company including developing
operational framework, processes, KPIs and developed the
Sharepoint structure. I have worked freelance for the majority
of my working life and after an earlier redundancy had set
up an IT recruitment firm with two colleagues which we
subsequently sold as our lives went in different directions.

Why did you decide to have a career change after becoming a mum?

I returned to work after my twins were born but struggled with
long commutes, long working hours and the exhaustion of

juggling ongoing sleepless nights, as neither of my boys were keen to sleep, combined with the challenge of delivering on fast-paced projects.

I was clearly trying to do too much as in 2012 I ended up in hospital in early stage organ failure caused by pneumonia with sepsis. The Consultant told me I was lucky my husband had got me to A&E on the Saturday evening because it was likely I would not have made Monday morning had I stayed at home. I was unable to work for over 12 months and during this time I settled my boys into primary school before attempting a part-time contract that quickly became full-time. I soon realised that I was no longer happy commuting but had no idea what other options I could consider.

Did you struggle to make the transition to business owner?

The crunch point came when my childcare collapsed overnight and I was forced to reassess options immediately. With very little thought I "knocked up" a logo, bought some cheap business cards and set up as a VA (Virtual Assistant) with no idea as to what services I would offer, to who or how much I would charge. After many years of working freelance I felt this was going to be an easy transition however I quickly identified some huge gaps in my knowledge that had a big impact on my business growth and confidence.

I received a recommendation to work with someone who was hugely knowledgeable and had a programme of support for entrepreneurs that helped them build successful businesses. The content was great, but I took this on just as I discovered one of my sons was having serious problems with bullying and he was struggling to cope. I wasn't totally focused on the course and as a result didn't maximise the learning opportunities which led the leader to have a very negative view of my commitment to my business and me. I felt deflated as I was struggling to meet her expectations and failing, while trying to juggle so many different facets of my life.

My son's problems were significant and after assessment it was apparent he needed lots of help which was unavailable due to government cuts, so I had to suddenly find a way to help my son deal with the mental health crisis he was experiencing. I retreated from my business purely keeping it ticking over, didn't set any goals and barely earned any money as I wanted to be available at a moment's notice for him. It was a terrifying time and I had many sleepless nights, my self-confidence plummeted and I felt like a failure – why had I not seen his anguish, why had I not protected him? I felt guilty for being preoccupied with my own goals and business, and worried that it was this that had caused his problems. Hindsight always enables a clearer view.

Taking this step back has paid off as my son is now happier, coping much better with life and the challenges faced during his transition to high school were much less than I expected. In October 2019 he told me he was happier than he had ever been before and I sobbed with relief. Success comes in many forms – this will forever be the biggest success of my life!

Was there a lightbulb moment or a turning point where it all "clicked" for you?

In 2019, my son's confidence was growing, the boys transitioned to high school and I found myself with 3.5 hours extra per day. The loss of the school run, the boys' growing independence and the freedom this had given was the trigger for a lot of personal change. I had started to fall out of love with my VA business earlier in the year, while the clients were fun, I wasn't enjoying the tasks, the work and felt I was missing something. I wanted to work differently using the tech and analytic skills I had developed in my earlier career but couldn't see how that would look or be attractive to potential clients. I had developed a detailed understanding of GDPR and how it is entwined in every element of the business processes but yet so many businesses were missing elements of it from the way they worked.

A colleague had been suggesting for sometime that I should change my business and focus on delivering a different set of services but I had resisted, partly as I was worried about making commitments and not delivering "just in case" I missed something with my son again. I now realise that I had lost confidence in myself because my life had been governed for so long by fear, worry and stress. Also I knew that there were people who had developed a very negative view of me which had left me anxious about putting myself "out there" again.

It was over lunch with a colleague that involved me outlining how she could use systems that worked together in her business to make life easier that I realised that this was what I wanted to do and went home deeply thoughtful.

What does success look like to you?

Success is hearing my son tell me he is happy with life after such dark days.

Success is seeing my boys transition to the next stage in their lives with confidence, excitement and with relative ease.

Success is the flexibility to take an afternoon off for lunch with my husband.

Success is clients who achieve business growth and confidence through the strategic implementation of new processes, systems and toolsets to streamline their business.

Success is replacing my full-time salary through running my business and achieving the goals I have set for myself.

How does your work/life balance look?

Balance and self-care are, and always have been, a huge challenge for me. Prior to marriage and children I loved my demanding job and the long hours, and used my free time to study work-related topics just for fun combined with buying semi-derelict houses to fix up. I still have a desire to push myself hard and have lots of things I want to achieve but experience has taught me that the long slow route is much safer, so I have parked some of my goals temporarily while I focus on other priorities for now, and I have recognised that I can still achieve them at a later date.

Luckily I rarely get ill but the pneumonia and sepsis in 2012 and, in 2019, another sudden acute and life-threatening illness were warning signs that I need to focus more on me and my health. 2019 was also the year I realised I was older than my Mum when she first went to the doctor about symptoms that were later identified as the cancer that killed her. The combination of these factors has ensured that I have, for the first time ever, included personal wellbeing goals in my 2020 targets.

I was born with hip dysplasia which led to major surgery involving a bone graft in my mid 20s and as a result have never walked or exercised without varying degrees of pain. This has led to difficulties enjoying sport as it was often painful to participate or painful afterwards and, despite a gym membership, avoided exercising often or with any intensity. 2020 will be the year this finally gets sorted. In late 2019 I started to work with a Sports Therapist to help me to resolve the problems and after three short sessions I have already started to feel the difference and am enjoying pain-free longer walks and sessions in the gym. Another significant success achieved in such a short period too.

What does a typical work day look like for you?

We are a house of early risers – my husband is out of the house by 7am and the boys leave around 7.15 to go to school. I do love a 5am start as I am most creative and productive earlier in the day but I don't do this on a regular basis. Once the chaos of the pre work, preschool breakfast dash has finished I frequently sit and have a quiet coffee, check in with friends, social media and make notes or to do lists for the day.

Other than that no two days are the same – meetings, networking, clients, dog walking, supermarket, laundry,

"Don't be afraid to make mistakes - these will be your greatest learning opportunities"

Jo Brianti

deliveries, working from the gym, exercising, cooking, dinner with my husband all get squeezed into the day. Some days there are sacrifices and often a need to reprioritise or refocus energies elsewhere, some days I sit down with a glass of wine/ dinner wondering how I got so much achieved. There are times when I suddenly realise the boys are home and I haven't moved from my desk all day as I have got engrossed or ended up down a rabbit hole of research/learning/reading.

I rarely work late into the evening at my desk, it is not my sweet spot although I may read, catch up on bookmarked websites I want to look at and sometimes Candy Crush is just the tonic after a day of dashing round.

How important has it been to have the right support and what impact has having that support had on your business and success?

Support is essential in all areas of life but for a long time it was difficult to talk about the problems I was dealing with as I felt so tired and very much like an overwhelmed rabbit in the headlights. I also wasn't ready to admit I felt I had failed and struggled with that feeling for a long time, with hindsight I know there was no way of knowing what was going on and what matters is the future.

I am now part of several on/offline networking groups that each bring different types of support to my life. The Cocoon is one of my favourite groups as it is full of women just like me juggling the many different elements of their life. It is a place where I know I am guaranteed to find a friendly ear, suggested solutions for problems or sometimes on difficult days just a non judgemental shoulder to cry on.

A friend and I established a local networking group for micro businesses to come together informally to build community, friendships and support. We recently celebrated one year in business together and it is proving to be a new challenge but is helping us to support our local network.

I am also lucky to have great friends who it is easy to enjoy time out with away from work which is also essential.

If you had your time again, is there anything you would do differently?

This sounds like such a cliché, but life is very short and we only get a single chance at it. It would be easy to look at the business progress I have made and think that I have failed but I have learnt so much about myself, my priorities (these do get blurred/dim as a parent), my needs/wants and where I am prepared to compromise. "Life is what happens to you while you are busy making other plans" is a line in a song by John Lennon and it is a favourite quote of mine – make plans, have goals/targets/ambitions but be flexible.

Play the long game, enjoy the process and don't be afraid to step back if you need to – business will still be there and starting over isn't such a bad thing.

Organise a session at the after-school club, or take the afternoon off to have a long boozy lunch with your husband if that's what suits you sometimes. Taking time out to reconnect with your partner is an important part of your wellbeing especially as they will be your biggest champion.

Lastly, COMPARISONITIS will cripple you, stifle your creativity and damage your self-esteem/confidence – don't do it. Remember the tale of the Hare and the Tortoise!

What's next for you?

In December 2019 I closed my VA business, shut down the website, took Christmas off work completely and started January 2020 with no clients and no plan but a headful of ideas for a new direction.

I started working on the process of crafting a business that would support delivery of my professional goals, bring me personal satisfaction and utilise more of my skills and knowledge. It has been a cathartic process as I have reviewed everything in my business and it has also been tough to analyse the good, the bad and the very ugly elements of what I have been doing including my own personal failures, but I have learnt so much and my new business will be stronger for it. Over the course of the next three months I will start to implement the changes, some gradually, some more radically and immediately such as taking down the website. 2020 will be the year all the learning comes together and my business plans are focused on delivering the growth I want.

I started mentoring in 2019 and was accepted as a Mentor with a national charity called BelEve. I started working with my first mentee in January 2020. Additionally, I have been accepted as a Business Mentor with the University of Surrey to work with their undergraduates who are seeking support to establish new businesses. This will be a growth area for me in 2020.

Jo's Top Tips:

1. Don't be afraid to make mistakes – these will be your greatest learning opportunities.

2. Don't feel you need to live up to other people's expectations or achieve at the same pace – everyone has their own unique drivers, be proud to be yourself.

3. Don't give up – taking a step back if needed gives you breathing space to focus on key priorities – it is not a weakness, but a sign of strength.

Key Takeaway

FELICITY SANDFORD

Business Name: Amazing Futures Ltd.
Website: www.amazingfutures.co.uk

Felicity runs a social media and
marketing agency, Amazing Futures
Ltd. She also runs two networking
groups and trains people to use social media
better for themselves or takes over the management
of social media accounts for those who would
rather outsource.

What did you do for a living before having children?

I was very much a corporate marketer. I started off my career,
fairly late in my mid 20s, having spent a few years after
university traveling and not taking life very seriously. I then
moved to London and got a role as a graduate marketing
trainee with KPMG. From there I went on to be a Senior
Marketing Executive with Reed Elsevier before getting a role
as UK and Ireland Marketing Communications Manager with
a building insulation company, where I managed a small team.
It was a role which required a lot of travel which was great fun
before children but less practical afterwards, although I went
back part-time after having my daughter.

Why did you decide to have a career change after becoming a mum?

I didn't immediately. I went back to work part-time shortly
after my daughter turned one. I had had a bad late pregnancy
with severe pre-eclampsia and my viewpoint on life had
changed. My daughter and I were lucky to be healthy, lucky to
be alive even and I wanted to spend as much time with her as

I could. I did not however want to give up working as I really craved that adult and brain engagement time too. I was now only working two and a half days so it was no longer feasible to manage a team. I still had to travel a bit and generally it was ok – but it was quite dull and I felt like they were making up work for me to do. I was pregnant again not long after I returned (oops!) and was back on maternity leave less than 12 months afterwards! Then when my son was about three months old, I spotted an advert for a nanny agency franchise which would allow you to work from home. I made the phone call, really took to Betty, the Franchisor, and from there took my first step into self-employment.

Did you struggle to make the transition to business owner?

I was lucky in a few respects. Betty was amazing. She had an existing franchisee who had run the West London branch for over a decade but had stepped down over a year ago due to ill health. Inspired by a university friend who asked his employer if they would like to make him redundant, I did exactly the same. I knew that there wasn't a lot of work for me in the new, slightly "made-up role." I also knew that they were making job cuts anyway but that as one of the only female managers in the company, they'd probably hesitate to put me in line for redundancy whilst on maternity leave. So basically it was voluntary redundancy – I just gave the first nudge! The redundancy pay was enough to buy the nanny agency with a fair chunk left to pay for most of our new kitchen – result!

My income has been very up and down since I became self-employed. I've had several months where I earned substantially over the maximum I ever earned as an employed marketing manager working for a huge, well known company. Other months I have earned considerably less and only really covered my outgoings – accountant, bookkeeper, Xero, memberships, subscriptions etc.

"It felt like a huge step, but within months of running the agency, when the first clients started paying and I was working around my son's naps and daughter's nursery slots fairly comfortably. I knew I'd made the right decision."

I will say that I am helped by the fact that my husband has a steady job and income that can provide for us comfortably as a family. My money does go towards the extras we want in life though – more holidays, towards our plan to move to a bigger house and other luxuries. I do think you need to work out how you will survive the lean months as, depending on what sort of business you do, it can be a bit boom and bust. On the whole though I am very happy with the income I am making considering I work so flexibly and take off a lot of time to be with the kids during the school holidays.

Was there a lightbulb moment or a turning point where it all "clicked" for you?
It took me months of deliberating and discussing with my husband, family and friends. It felt like a huge step, but within months of running the agency, when the first clients started paying and I was working around my son's naps and daughter's nursery slots fairly comfortably. I knew I'd made the right decision.

What does success look like to you?
To me, it's setting yourself new goals all the time and ticking those off one by one. It is continuing to find your work rewarding and not sitting back, but constantly upping the goals and setting yourself new challenges. It isn't necessarily all

about income although my goals for next year are much more income-based as I have had several years of upskilling now in digital marketing and it's time to reap the rewards!

How does your work/life balance look?

Hmm, it could be better – I do spend too many late nights working. That said, I'm a Night Owl and always have been. My children are both in school and do several after-school clubs on-site, which they love, so that makes things easier, but I am around for other activities they need to be taken to, be that swimming lessons, tennis or judo that they can't do after school. I'm there for every school concert, class assembly, sports day and science fair pretty much.

I love that my children can select the clubs they want to do in the holidays – rather than it having to be the ones with the longest hours. I also love that I can go back with them to Wales frequently in the school holidays so they get lots of time with their grandparents and a lovely balance between London and countryside life. I am a mum AND an entrepreneur and I am proud of that!

Last year my daughter participated in a London schools' poetry slam with two of her classmates after being selected from school auditions. To watch her perform in a Central London theatre, I had to take an entire day off work. It's highly unlikely I could have taken the day off for it in a corporate role with annual leave being so restricted, but being self-employed I could. Just as well because they won! Seeing her recite a poem she had written so confidently, in front of 800 school children, teachers and parents, was wonderful. Hearing the thunderous applause and the excited chanting of her school friends after the winner's announcement, made every late night working 100% worthwhile! I would have hated to have missed that.

How important has it been to have the right support and what impact has having that support had on your business and success?

The Cocoon business club launch came just in time for me setting up my second business, Amazing Futures. I was one of the founding members and at the time I was in the process of selling my nanny agency franchise and getting ready to set up my marketing business. I had started studying for the Google Squared Online diploma in digital leadership and getting things in place. Setting up your own business from scratch is very different to buying a franchise (although that was a fantastic learning experience too). I suddenly had to consider things like whether to go limited or stay as a sole trader, how to get my new website done, contracts etc. The Cocoon, even in its very early days, was an invaluable source of information. I can't tell you how useful it was to have a safe space to bounce ideas for company names with!

I have also had some mentoring which has helped keep me on track. For the last three years I have worked from a local (cheap and cheerful, nothing fancy) co-working office which I also highly recommend. It's lovely to have "colleagues" again and I feel far more focused working from there than from home, or a coffee shop.

I have made some fantastic friends through being a business owner. It is so worth going out to events and meetups to network – and joining membership communities like The Cocoon. You never know where your next fabulous collaboration could come from. In the last two years I have collaborated with Erin herself and another fabulous business lady – Sara Tateno of Happity in the Activity Providers Academy – in creating an online course for children's activity providers. I have also set up two networking groups – including with another Cocoon Member, Jo Brianti. As the Ealing Business Buddies, we host face-to-face meet-ups and training workshops for West London business owners and freelancers.

"If the work isn't flexible enough to fit around the needs and lives of my children, then it isn't the right kind of work for me."

Felicity Sandford

#MumpreneurEvolution

If you had your time again, is there anything you would do differently?

Probably not a lot because every mistake I've made has taken me down a different, but ultimately beneficial track. I would certainly track my costs better though (still room for improvement there!) as I have wasted a fair bit of money along the way.

I love being a mumpreneur. I take my business very seriously and I am passionate about it in a way I never was about my corporate career. However, I do not lose sight of the reason why I started it in the first place. If the work isn't flexible enough to fit around the needs and lives of my children, then it isn't the right kind of work for me.

What's next for you?

I am about to embark on the Emma Van Heusen Facebook Ads Strategist course, widely regarded as the best of its kind. It will be three months of hard graft but I'm looking forward to upping my game and hopefully my prices to match!

Felicity's Top Tips:

1. Find your tribe as early as possible – the sooner you have a support network of other entrepreneurs who "get it" the better!

2. Invest or accept family/ friends help with childcare early on if you can and don't feel guilty about it.

3. Invest in your own self development as much as you can reasonably afford – join The Cocoon for support and learning.

Key Takeaway

_____

_____

_____

_____

_____

_____

_____

NINA MUCALOV

Business Name: Nina Mucalov Photography
Website: www.ninamucalov.com

Nina is a lifestyle family and
personal brand photographer
based in London. Her passion is
showing women what a beautiful job they are doing
– whether it's mums with their families or female
entrepreneurs with their businesses (or both!). Her
photographs tell your story and help you see your life
or business in a new light.

What did you do for a living before having children?

Before having children I worked in the world of investments
and hedge funds. I worked in both big name and boutique
firms and was very often the only senior woman on my team.
I loved my job. But I also knew that I eventually wanted to
do something more creative and that gave me the flexibility I
needed to create the life I truly desired. Three years after going
back to work, and after my second child, I knew it was time to
make the leap.

Why did you decide to have a career change after becoming a mum?

I fell in love with photography almost a decade ago. It was
after seeing my wedding photographs, and how they were in
a different league to the photos I had become accustomed to
from iPhones. I became obsessed with learning everything I
could to create images that captured the true beauty of people
and moments and details. Fast forward almost eight years and I
am now photographing dozens of families and female business

owners each year. I love capturing images that mums are proud to share whilst helping them take their businesses to the next level.

Did you struggle to make the transition to business owner?

Yes! Photography is something I love! I do it in any spare moment. I read books about it, I dream about it, I take classes on it in my free time. But at first it felt somehow 'wrong' to charge money for something that I am so passionate about. I also suffered doubts. Was my work good enough to be charging? What if my clients didn't love their galleries? What if I couldn't find any clients? But I came to realise that I was providing a valuable service. And doing it for free wasn't doing anyone any favours. As soon as I started charging for my shoots the people I was photographing valued it more and I, in turn, valued myself more. I fell in love with the business side of photography as much as the creative side.

Was there a lightbulb moment or a turning point where it all "clicked" for you?

Becoming visible and offering my services vocally and on social media was something I struggled with initially, but through coaching, and working on my confidence I have learned to love marketing and selling and all things social media.
I know it's how I get my message out to the people I set up my business to serve. And I know that serving these mothers and entrepreneurs is WAY more important than worrying what my school friend's husband might be thinking or saying about my Facebook posts.

What does success look like to you?

Success to me is having a daily/weekly/monthly schedule that works for me and for our family. It's having the time I need to take care of myself so I am able to be the mum, wife, friend, sister, photographer that I enjoy being. Success is reaching the goals I set in terms of income and the number of clients I am able to serve as well as growing creatively and feeling positive about where I am in my business. It is helping a mother see the beauty that her sleepless nights (and sometimes endless days) are creating and helping female entrepreneurs feel confident by increasing their visibility online with photographs they are proud to share. Delivering these images and receiving incredible feedback makes me feel successful every time.

Prior to launching my own business I was a Portfolio Manager at a boutique investment firm. I definitely took a salary cut when launching my own business (my target income for the first year of my business was about the same as what I earned in a month in my corporate job).

Having said that, through all the work I have been doing on my money mindset I now feel more abundance around money than I ever have. I am smashing my initial goals and can now see a future where I am matching or earning more than I was in my corporate life.

How does your work/life balance look?

I work on average 20-30 hours per week. I have a general structure to my weeks (Mondays sales & marketing, Tuesdays Creative, Wednesdays finances & tech & tasks, Thursdays Creative, Friday photoshoots, Saturday morning photoshoots) But also the flexibility to move things around when needed. My youngest daughter has a lot of extra medical appointments and having the flexibility to move my weeks around to accommodate these has taken a lot of stress out of my life. It also means I have the flexibility to get in a few hours of extra sleep during the day in the weeks when my husband is out of town and I am parenting solo.

What does a typical work day look like for you?

A typical day is a funny one – it changes week-by-week – but here are a few of mine:

Example day #1 (typical Monday)
- 9–11am: Local coffee shop for early morning emails, work on client galleries etc
- 11–12pm: Speech therapy appointment with my 4 year old daughter
- 12–2pm: Lunch, errands & tasks around home
- 2–5pm: Work on my bed at home: editing galleries, social media, project work
- 5pm–7.30: Kid's dinner, bath-time, stories etc

Example day #2 (typical Friday)
- 8–11am: Early morning branding photoshoot with a client
- 11–12pm: Decompress after my photoshoot with a hot chocolate and journalling or meditation
- 12–2pm: 1st edit of a gallery and answer most important emails
- 3–6pm: School run + homework + dinner + tidy up
- 6–7.30pm: Retreat to my room while my hubby puts the kids to bed
- 7.30–10pm: Settle in on the sofa with a G&T, take-away and Netflix

How important has it been to have the right support and what impact has having that support had on your business and success?

Support has been SO important! Being a part of an online membership (The Cocoon), has meant I've had a community to go to to to ask (silly) questions of, to celebrate my wins with and to learn from, whether they're one step ahead of me or ten steps ahead of me. Being an entrepreneur comes with its unique set of joys and challenges and having a community of people (women!) who understand this has been invaluable. Coaching and mentoring one-to-one has also been a game-changer for me. I'm called-out on the stories I'm telling myself, and that are holding me back. I have someone cheering me on when I'm feeling discouraged and someone to help me see things from a different point of view, pick myself up and keep moving forward when, on my own, I might have been tempted to give up. I know that my business wouldn't be where it is today without both of these kinds of help..

If you had your time again, is there anything you would do differently?

I love where I am in my business and in my life, so it's hard to think about doing things differently. One thing I might do is invest in coaching earlier. It has helped my business more than I could have imagined. Having that support in the early months when things can be their trickiest, and when doubts are running rampant, would have been invaluable.

What's next for you?

My plan is to grow my business and my client-base particularly for my personal branding photography. I love working with other female business owners. I love seeing how professional quality images can be a driving factor in increasing their visibility, their impact and their business bottom line. I'm excited to be doing more of that.

Nina's Top Tips:

1. Join an entrepreneur group (I joined The Cocoon within the first few months of launching my business and am so glad I did!)

2. Build a positive mindset around money (Cori Javid's work is amazing!)

3. Celebrate all your successes! The big ones and the tiny ones.

Key Takeaway

_____

_____

_____

_____

_____

_____

_____

_____

_____

TANYA BUNTING

Business Name: Tanya Bunting
Coaching
Website: www.tanyabuntingcoaching.org

Tanya describes herself as an early year's practitioner at heart and at the time of writing wonders if she'll be the oldest mumpreneur in the book! After 17 years as a school leader, she discovered NLP and decided to discover its potential within and beyond the classroom. Tanya is now a Personal Development Coach with Clinical Hypnotherapy and NLP in her toolbox. Her core purpose is to support others to accelerate progress towards their goals.

What did you do for a living before having children?

Before having children, I was a student and carried our first baby Stephen (now aged 29) throughout my PGCE year. When he was three months old, I took up my first teaching post. Five and a half years later, I'd given birth to Jenni-Lou and interviewed successfully for the post of Deputy Headteacher at a local first school. Jenni-Lou was a bundle of surprises. To cut a long story short, she has Down Syndrome and required a life-saving operation at birth and subsequent operations more or less yearly until she was ten years old. Like most children, she fitted into our working and family life, and I survived life as a working mum with the practical support of my parents who were grandparents in a million. They supported with childcare on a daily basis throughout the schooling years, and my Mum still supports Jenni-Lou on a regular basis now.

Why did you decide to have a career change after becoming a mum?

After 28 years of teaching, 17 of which were in school leadership, I decided to take a career break. During the first six weeks, I completed my first NLP Practitioner qualification after which I signed up with a supply agency with the sole purpose of going back to class to realise its potential in the classroom. After 13 years, stepping back to class was a daunting prospect.

On the first day with my Early Years foundation Class, I honestly wondered whether I would make it to breaktime. But within minutes, I felt like I'd fallen in love all over again. I loved teaching and had never found life in the classroom so easy. Not only could I focus on teaching without the pressure of school leadership, but I had a completely new skillset that enabled me to manage myself and the children more effectively than ever before. The parents, children and my colleagues noticed a tangible difference in my classroom compared to others; and whilst some of them speculated on what was different, the subtle application of NLP enabled subtle tweaks that made the biggest difference.

I loved being a classroom teacher during the week and using my weekends to study and achieve the new qualifications that I have now. Using my new skills on myself in the first instance, enabled me to attain a Clinical Qualification including a postgraduate certificate during the most challenging years in my life so far. That is to say that NLP enabled me to study, care and move to a new house simultaneously. I enjoyed the privilege of continuing to care for Jenni, as well as supporting

"Within minutes, I felt like I'd fallen in love all over again. I loved teaching and had never found life in the classroom so easy."

my parents throughout my Dad's "Alzheimer Years" and subsequent death. On the morning of my Dad's first anniversary, I completed my final presentation to become an NLP Trainer. Thereafter, I "NLP'd" myself (with a bit of help from John La Valle, President of the Society of NLP) to leave the classroom.

Did you struggle to make the transition to business owner?

The transition from being fully self-employed to being a full-time business owner was exciting on one hand and daunting on the other. Whilst I knew I had the practical skills to secure change for my clients, establishing my own brand and marketing myself was a completely new ball game that I'm continuing to learn. And, to niche or not to niche continues to be the question! Almost a year after becoming fully self-employed, my business continues to build at a manageable rate. I have yet to earn the equivalent of my Headteacher salary. That said, my hourly rate exceeds what I earned as a school leader and my clients are happy with the value I provide.

There are still days when I wonder if I'm putting my focus on the aspects that have the biggest impact and I'm still a work in progress with learning and developing my digital marketing skills. As an NLP Master Practitioner and trainer, I manage my own self-doubt and support others to do the same. I'm eternally grateful to my teachers and mentors, specifically Dr Richard Bandler, whose technology has enabled me to manage my own state and develop my learning skills to manage a successful career change in a relatively short space of time.

Was there a lightbulb moment or a turning point where it all "clicked" for you?

The lightbulb moment for me came when I realised that if I could achieve one of my own big goals four years sooner than I originally thought possible, I could support others to do the same. I'm pleased to say that I haven't looked back; so much so that the more my clients achieve, the more I want to help them achieve more and so it goes on!

What does success look like to you?

Success for me is achieving any step that moves me or my clients in the right direction. It can be as small as the latest social media post or as big as a client achieving a goal that they doubted was possible. I measure my success on a daily basis via my action plan and "to do" list, as well as through client reviews and money in the bank! As a reflector, I consistently and insistently note the strategies that work and where I can improve to achieve the quickest change. If honest, I'm discerning about which clients I agree to work with. Change work takes time and energy beyond the coaching or therapy room, so there are times when I actively limit my clients in order to have the time and space to prepare myself to be in the right place for them. I am proud and privileged to work with clients of all ages to address all sorts of issues.

At the time of writing, my client base ranges in age from five to 70, all of whom are on track to overcome issues such as anxiety, depression, pain and habits. I'm not sure that I can fully reflect in words the feeling associated with the job satisfaction of supporting others to reach their goals so I'll leave it up to the reader to imagine how good it feels when a young person reduces or eliminates a tic, a mum gives birth easily or an addict is smoke or alcohol-free and enjoying life beyond their addiction. And that's to name but a few!

How does your work/life balance look?

My work life balance is possibly a work/work balance that works for me! I've always given 110% towards the task in hand and that's not changed. The difference now is that I can manage my schedule as I see fit. I can prioritise time to work in, on or beyond the business, or to enjoy dedicated family time. If something crops up, I can take my foot off the pedal knowing that I can accelerate again when the time is right. When I'm at my best, my day starts with a positive routine that includes meditation, reading, writing and exercise. When I keep my own reservoir full, I'm more productive. At the time of writing, I've intentionally taken time out of my schedule to deal with an unexpected challenge and whilst I've known the risk, having the skills to make an informed decision without the worry and concern that I may have exhibited in the past is liberating.

How important has it been to have the right support and what impact has having that support had on your business and success?

A significant challenge for me has been coping with the loneliness of running my own business. As a headteacher, there were times when I felt lonely because there were aspects of my job that only I could deal with. As a sole trader, I'm now on my "own" as a businesswoman for much of the time. As a headteacher, I never used social media and now I'm as "at risk" as the next person of using my phone for company.

I'm pleased to say that business networking, a supervisor/coach and an accountability partner have all helped enormously as I've become increasingly more familiar with my new identity and the associated issues. Whilst I'm a good self-challenger, if I articulate my goals, milestones and timescales to trusted colleagues, I'm far more likely to focus, prioritise and stay on track. I'm proud and privileged to be a member of the trainer support teams for Paul McKenna and Dr Richard Bandler, which means that I still get to work with a team (not least one of the BEST teams) up to six times per year. This gives me a huge incentive to be my best and to manage my time in between the seminars to achieve maximum results.

If you had your time again, is there anything you would do differently?

It's early days so it's difficult to say what I would do if I had my time again. At the time of writing, my aim is to ensure my own clinic/office for completing local work in the near future. This is simply to eliminate the task of booking a room for each and every consultation. That said, I adore the freedom of going wherever my work takes me: Bournemouth, Southampton, Central London, Orlando and beyond. If I could turn the clock back, I would have learnt NLP before completing my first degree and would encourage EVERYBODY else to do the same. NLP has enabled me to think differently and achieve more.

What's next for you?

What's next for me includes publishing my first book and an associated course that encompasses all of my skills developed to date, as well as developing opportunities to teach new subjects to new audiences. If someone had told me six years ago that I would be a hypnotist, running my own business and leading change beyond the classroom, it would have been beyond my wildest dreams. With the support of a loving family and a dollop of cash to fund my training, I can now enjoy the freedom, variety and flexibility that self-employment can give.

I'm still a teacher and a learner at heart. I now get to teach new skills to discerning people (young or old) who want to gain control over their own destiny. I LOVE my job and the associated rewards. Maintaining a continuous flow of clients and course delegates is an on-going challenge; when I find the solution, I'll be sure to share it!

Tanya's Top Tips:

1. Ensure that your core purpose continues to be something you love. Believe in yourself. As Walt Disney said, "If you can dream it, you can do it."

2. Establish a working week that enables you to work, parent and play in whatever way is best for you to fill your reservoir.

3. Set manageable goals and allow yourself time to enjoy the intrinsic and external rewards along the way. In other words, learn NLP and transform your future.

Key Takeaway

_____

_____

_____

_____

_____

_____

_____

_____

CARLY ROSE

Business Name: Carly Rose, Online
Business Management
Website: www.carlyroseva.co.uk

Carly is an experienced Personal Assistant, and
worked with key figureheads mainly in the public
sector, specialising in education. She now offers her
services to businesses that are expanding and in need
of some support with day-to-day tasks. Expansion
and demand have meant Carly now manages many
of her clients' entire online business operations,
including social media.

What did you do for a living before having children?

I have always worked as a Personal Assistant in differing areas
of the public sector, and particularly enjoyed my job as PA to
the Headteacher in a large secondary school.

Why did you decide to have a career change after becoming a mum?

Life totally changed and so did my priorities. I persevered but
bounced around between different part-time jobs. I constantly
suffered guilt from all directions. Firstly the classic 'mama
guilt' for leaving my child whilst I went to work, coupled with
the feeling of dread when I had to let work down when my
baby was ill or had an appointment. Furthermore, my Dad
had terminal cancer around that time, which resulted in me
taking some compassionate leave. I found it tough to rediscover
a sense of purpose in the workplace. Once my second son
arrived I decided that the rigid and inflexible part-time roles
were just not going to work for me and my family anymore,

so whilst on maternity leave I tentatively started my online business.

Did you struggle to make the transition to business owner?

I never considered myself a business owner in the beginning! I viewed the work as something I was trying out, almost with the mindset of a hobby, in order to keep myself busy. I have always felt confident in my own abilities and have an incredibly supportive husband and family so I was lucky enough not to fear failure, however what I was frightened about was putting myself out there in the online space. For this reason I controlled the growth of my business. I told myself I should build slowly because of the children. I had lots of PA experience but no official qualifications to run an online business, so why would people pay for my services? Other questions I asked myself included whether there was even a need in the market for what I was offering? Was the market saturated? I later discovered these were all stories I was telling myself and limiting beliefs that I needed to work through.

Was there a lightbulb moment or a turning point where it all "clicked" for you?

I set myself some clear goals and when I reached these with ease, I quickly realised that I was running a real business. After that I seemed to be attracting clients without any advertising, which meant that all of a sudden I was fully booked. It was at this point that I decided I needed to stop using the children as an excuse for not making a genuine success of my creation. I had a full roster of clients whose businesses were growing, which resulted in my workload increasing, and lots of word-of-mouth recommendations. This was really happening! This was my job now!

Like any business starting from scratch I was concerned that I wouldn't make any money or it would be hard. My first goal was to match my maternity allowance so that when this stopped it wouldn't matter. I reached this gradually and then the figure I set my sights on was £1000 a month. This figure to me felt like I was the real deal…4 figures! A real business woman!! I would be able to contribute again towards bills and have some left for me. I was so excited when I first reached this, and in the following nine months I managed to double it, surpassing any previous salary I'd had working full-time. I am now looking at outsourcing to my associates team in order to keep this income consistent but give me back some time for that work life balance we all desire.

What does success look like to you?

Success is such a personal thing and honestly, I already feel successful. Still, running a business is stressful, and there are days when I panic that I don't have enough time to manage the juggling act between work and life. When this happens, I always stop, take a breath and remember that I am so lucky. I work fewer hours than I ever did before children, yet I earn more money. I never miss a school pick up, concert, nativity or swimming lesson. I get to be mummy whilst still allowing myself to go for coffee with my girlfriends on a Monday morning (the best therapy!). I get to go to my fitness bootcamp four times a week. I feel happy and, for me, happiness and success are very much interconnected. The feeling I get after a busy week helping other mums-in-business is amazing. My clients are all incredible and to be a part of their team, assisting them in their successes, provides me with a wonderful sense of job satisfaction.

How does your work/life balance look?

I work around 25 hours a week and some of these hours are on a Sunday evening. Lots of people ask if this bothers me. The answer is no! I *CHOOSE* to work Sunday so I can meet a girlfriend for lunch during the week, or take an hour out of my schedule to go shopping. I work around the school run and pre-

"Decide, believe and take action."

Carly Rose

school hours. I'm also lucky enough to have two very helpful Nanas! There are days where work overflows into the time I am with the children, and this is when I feel most stressed. I think it is important that the boys see that mummy works but not at the expense of the attention they deserve growing up. It is not fair on them, me or the client. I have to work hard at maintaining balance and avoiding overwhelm.

What does a typical work day look like for you?

I sometimes wonder if I have had a typical day as a mum and business owner… something ALWAYS comes up to change the day I had planned out for myself!!

My day usually starts at 5:30 when I head out to my 6am bootcamp. This is essential me-time and I always come home with good energy for the day ahead and in a good frame of mind. I arrive home just as the rest of the household is getting up so the morning mayhem begins of breakfast and getting everyone out the door for school and pre-school. I have usually thrown a wash on and cleaned a bathroom or whipped the hoover round by this point too! I aim to start my work day at 9:30 (so 10am then!!) I start by checking all channels of communication with my team and clients; email, Slack, Asana and Trello to see if anything urgent has come up. I then refer to my daily list of ToDo's. I use Asana for recurring tasks but I always end my work day jotting down any ad hoc tasks in my planner for the next day. I find that if it isn't written down it doesn't get done! I aim to do two hour chunks of work and

"I sometimes wonder if I have had a typical day as a mum and business owner… something ALWAYS comes up to change the day I had planned out for myself!"

then take short breaks but this doesn't leave much time before school pickup so I often go back to some tasks of an evening, especially if I have met with a client or friend. I try to be in mummy mode after school but it can be hard to switch off when I haven't completed that ToDo list and I often get to dinner and have forgotten to take something out of the freezer!! My husband is great once he gets home and often takes over and does the bedtime routine so I can get an hour's extra work in and we can enjoy an evening together.

How important has it been to have the right support and what impact has having that support had on your business and success?

Support is key, you have to feel like there is someone in your corner or somewhere to go to get that all-important advice. It is said that working for yourself can be lonely. I have to say I have never felt this! I am too busy and there are always people coming and going in my house. There are also so many groups online that you can join to find like-minded people to bounce ideas with or offload to on a bad day. That was the first thing I did when I was researching for my business: joined Facebook groups for Virtual Assistants and Online Business Managers. Definitely find yourself a business bestie! That one person that will keep you on track and accountable but also tell you everything is going to work out and that you are fabulous! I have completed mindset courses, masterminds and group coaching programs that have been incredibly helpful on my journey. There is so much available out there but it can be tricky not to get sucked in to doing *all* the courses and not actually just cracking on!

If you had your time again, is there anything you would do differently?

I'm not sure there is. I would have said that I should have stopped making excuses sooner but hindsight is a wonderful thing and actually I was just not ready to go all in... until I was!

What's next for you?

I have recently begun to outsource some of my workload and I intend to build on this in the next twelve months so that I can serve more clients or provide alternative services to mamas in business and take back a little more me-time. I would also like to be able to support other women in the future who are looking to become virtual assistants or online business managers by offering a mentoring program.

Carly's Top Tips:

1. Accept all offers of help. If, like me, you didn't feel able to accept help with business, accept help with the children, the housework, meals. Don't try and do *all the things*! You can't do it all by yourself.

2. Believe in yourself. You can do anything you decide you want to do. Decide, believe and take action.

3. Super practical and oh so important top tip: Have all your contracts in place right from the very start.

Key Takeaway

_____

_____

_____

_____

_____

_____

_____

_____

AMY HOBSON

Business name: Focus Your Future
and The Connexion for Women
in Business
Website: www.focusyourfuture.co.uk
and www.theconnexionfwib.co.uk

Amy Hobson has two business interests
which she works on around her family commitments.
She is a Digital Coach, Trainer and Speaker and
co-owner of an all-female networking business.

What did you do for a living before having children?

I worked for a nominee stock broker but made the decision
that, whilst I could progress, it wasn't a great environment for
flexible working and had long and unsociable hours. I knew
that I wanted to have a family so moved into franchising.
I stayed in franchising when I became a Mum and grew my
family, including owning my own franchise, working part-
time and then increasing my hours to full-time. I took over as
Franchise Operations Manager just after I had my fourth son.

Why did you decide to have a career change after becoming a mum?

After redundancy in 2015, due to a head office relocation,
I made the decision to work for myself. I had separated from
my husband in 2010 so had become a single parent when
my youngest was less than a year old. Working full-time with
four children was incredibly hard and I only survived with the
support of my parents who provided the bulk of my childcare
(I paid my Mum but not as much as childcare would have
cost me). When I was made redundant my boys were 12,

10, eight and five so I needed something that could be more flexible and allow me to be a Mum but still earn me a decent income. Employed work just didn't fit – I had been lucky with the franchise role as I had been able to build it around me but finding something similar was impossible.

Did you struggle to make the transition to business owner?

I think the hardest thing was self-doubt. I knew I could do it but there was always a niggling fear that I might not be able to. I was, and still am, sometimes caught between the dread of failure and the dread of having to fit it all in if I am successful! Working for yourself is great but it also comes with risks. Six months after I became self-employed I was really ill with gallstones and lost two months of work over Christmas and New Year. With no partner or husband as a financial backup that was a really, really scary place to be. I then spent a year struggling with ill-health but couldn't afford to take time off to recover properly. I've been employed since I was 14 so not having the safety net of holiday pay and sick pay was particularly difficult when it was such early days for my business. It also ultimately led to my decision to not have just one business interest so I could avoid putting all my eggs in one basket.

Was there a lightbulb moment or a turning point where it all "clicked" for you?

I don't think there was a specific lightbulb moment for me. It was more of a gradual realisation that if I didn't have faith in my own abilities then who would? With that faith I could trust my decisions and become much firmer, including turning down opportunities that just didn't feel quite right. It can be really hard to not only have faith in your abilities but also to then take action, trust your instincts and have confidence that you have made the right choice. Even if that choice is to say no to something, it's important that you believe you have made the correct decision.

I went into partnership with a lady I didn't know very well when we took over Connexions in May 2019. I had just started a new business interest and was in a busy period with my digital work but I just knew that it was the right thing to do. I'm so glad I listened to my instinct. It's still early days but we both love it and are growing the network! I wouldn't have done it a few years earlier as I would have talked myself out of it.

What does success look like to you?
My definition of success has definitely changed as I have got older. What I saw as successful in my 20's is definitely not where I am now but I do still see myself as successful in many ways. Would I like to develop my business and improve my income? Absolutely. Have I achieved everything I am capable of? Absolutely not. BUT (and it is a really important but) I am primarily a single Mum to four wonderful boys who still very much need me. Even my increasingly independent 17 year-old son still needs me to be there as his Mum and whilst in some ways it was harder to have four children under 8, I actually find parenting much harder now. The advantage of working for myself is that I can flex my businesses to fit around my family and that's a huge success for me. I would still really struggle to do it without my parents' support but I am incredibly proud of what I have achieved in the last few years.

My businesses all rely on my customers' success. Whether it is business growth through the digital strategy we have developed together, or really good connections being made at one of our

"The advantage of working for myself is that I can flex my businesses to fit around my family and that's a huge success for me."

meetings, I haven't succeeded unless they do. When I see their achievements and know that I have played a part, that is my real measure of success and it's that feeling that keeps me doing what I am doing.

How does your work/life balance look?

My work/life balance will always vary as my work can fluctuate. I definitely don't always get it right but I have learnt the hard way that burning the candle at both ends doesn't work for me or my boys. I've also learnt to look at the balance slightly differently. When I first became a single parent I felt like I needed to do everything to prove that I still could but in reality I struggled to make it work. I now avoid saying "I can't" and look at it as more of a choice. "I won't" or "I choose not to" is actually much more powerful and puts me in control of my time and my choices.

What does a typical work day look like for you?

I'd love to have an answer for this question but I don't think I ever have a typical work day. In general I do the school run most mornings and will then go to the office for as much time as I can. I worked from home for years but now rent a small office close to home. It's less than a five minute drive away but I am much more focussed when I am there and it means that I can walk away from work when I need to. I try to block my time around client meetings or calls. If I don't I can struggle to get everything done and it also helps me to prioritise. If I only have an hour before pick up then I need to get done what *has* to be done (even if I don't want to do it) rather than what I would *like* to do. I try and work as effectively as I can around the commitments that I have so every day varies. On a school pickup day, for example, I often schedule a call for when I am sat in the car waiting. I have to get there early to get parked so it makes sense to use that time to make client calls or some of the other "admin" that a family with four children seems to

"I have a brilliant coach who I love working with and who has made a real difference to my business and personal mindset but I may need a different kind of support in the future."

produce. When I am working away I try to travel by train so that I can work en route.

Although I am a digital coach I still have a paper planner that I use to manage practically everything. My client meetings and work are in there as well as my personal life, my ex husband's work schedule, my boyfriend's schedule, scout camps, appointments, holidays, birthdays, etc. etc. If it is a 'definite' and can't be changed then it's written in ink. If it might change, then it is written in pencil. I do use the free Cosi Calendar app for my boys so that they know who they are with during each week and where I am working if I am working away. Some days they will be with me and some days with my Mum or their Dad which can make it difficult to have what they need at the right house.

From the outside my working day and schedule can look pretty chaotic but it is structured and works for us as a close family and an extended, blended one.

How important has it been to have the right support and what impact has having that support had on your business and success?
It is so important to have the right support but I also think that you need to recognise that what you need may change during your business journey. I have a brilliant coach who I love working with and who has made a real difference to my business and personal mindset but I may need a different kind

of support in the future. Ongoing support through online forums is also invaluable as well as face-to-face meet ups if you can. Working on your own business day in and day out can be isolating, so meeting up with others regularly is essential not just to keep you sane but also sometimes for a different perspective on a problem or challenge you may be facing.

If you had your time again, is there anything you would do differently?

I would definitely have taken the plunge earlier. Redundancy made me make a decision that I probably would have put off as my personal circumstances made it unlikely that I could give up the safety net of paid employment. At the time I was horrified and felt completely unemployable. I felt that I could either be a Mum, or work for someone else, with nothing in between. But now, with hindsight, I'm glad it happened.

What's next for you?

Continuing to work on my businesses and to see them grow alongside my boys. As my family's needs continue to change then so will my businesses and I'm OK with that.

Amy's Top Tips:

1. Don't be afraid to go for it – success is usually just outside your comfort zone.

2. Your vibe attracts your tribe so be honest and make sure you are always working with people that are right for you.

3. Be prepared for the bad times and the good times. It's a roller-coaster but it's definitely worth it for the views at the top.

Key Takeaway

_____

_____

_____

_____

_____

_____

_____

_____

_____

_____

BONITA ELMS

Business name: Bonita Bakes
Website: www.bonitabakes.co.uk

Bonita Elms is a wedding cake baker/designer. She creates unique edible tiered centrepieces using inspiration from the gorgeous Dorset coastline and stunning natural beauty of the New Forest. Her aim is to ultimately reflect these elements in her designs working closely with her clients' ideas to create a unique and delicious wedding cake for a couple's special day.

What did you do for a living before having children?

An early interest in art, drawing & painting led me to study Fashion Design at Art College in Bournemouth. After my course, a small local women's retail fashion shop was looking for a window dresser which turned out to be one of those lightbulb moments – 'why not display clothes instead of making them?' This was enjoyable and fun paid work at last. It felt brilliant, to create a display and entice customers into a shop and it boosted my always red-faced shyness even if working on show behind clear window glass was a way of hiding.

The early 90's brought retail recessions but my determination to still work in Display kept me employed for over ten years. I worked for big companies like Etam, Snob, Evans, the Burton Group, BHS Home Stores and, my ultimate favourite, River Island, as a southwest Area Display Manager with a flashy company car. My working days were very long but totally immersive and enjoyable.

Why did you decide to have a career change after becoming a mum?

This busy working and travelling life became less important after meeting my best friend (later to become my husband) and the planned arrival of our 1st lil daughter, nearly 22 years ago. Soon after she was followed by her two, now towering, brothers.

After my daughter was born I had three months maternity leave before deciding whether I wanted to return to work. I did some freelance work for River Island during that time, but leaving my newborn baby girl even for the odd day was unbearable. I decided I wanted to be a full-time mum so that I could enjoy every day of exhausted fun, knowing that those early years are golden and will never return.

Looking back now, family life can be the best training for us as parents and as business owners. My decision to become a full-time mum (teacher,counsellor, mentor, nurse, 24-hour carer, cleaner, taxi driver (latest job) list goes on)… was a clear and definite, if not slightly, brave one. Above all, knowing our young family was our responsibility and being there, having fun and loving them like no-one else meant reaping big rewards (some skint at times) as each precious moment in their lives unfolded.

Building a family is similar to building a secure, strong foundation in any new business. Being a creative soul with a (slightly mad) sense of humour along with my loud hearty laugh meant my time with my children were often crazy at times but always a lot of fun. Teaching toddlers to bake is a crazy messy activity yet results were mostly edible which was a big win!

Did you struggle to make the transition to business owner?

At around the age of 12 years, to my surprise, the children suddenly became young adults. This meant a chance to sometimes relax and have time to ourselves.

I started to feel drawn to the lure of finding paid work again. I decided to become my own boss, baking for real paying clients, because it felt like a natural progression from what I was already doing. My cake-baking skills were certainly well practised over the years, they were definitely a factor in getting my job/life mojo back.

Was there a lightbulb moment or a turning point where it all "clicked" for you?

Following our gut feeling can sometimes create a series of events which involve meeting the right people just at the right time. A kind of 'stars are aligned' moment. Opportunities do happen, but making them happen is slightly better really.

So walking into a small local cake shop business, and somehow literally selling myself, landed me a perfect part-time little job as a cake baker for five years. All thanks to the kids (and hubby of course) for giving me the self-confidence to just grab those opportunities and not look back.

My current home-based wedding cake business evolved from a combination of my part-time work, my early arty interests, and from baking with my children. I see baking as a form of meditation, getting deliberately lost but focussed at the same time. It is a great feeling, with the added bonus of some tastings if baking for clients, or scoffing for the always-starving family!!

What does success look like to you?

Success used to mean a lovely level of monetary wealth, but now having experienced the richness of raising a family into strong individuals, for me means an amazingly better meaning of success! 'Good things come to those who wait' but they are more likely coming from the effort behind the scenes too – learning, working, making mistakes, finding solutions and the determination to keep going.

How does your work/life balance look?

I am lucky that my home is close to miles of beautiful sandy beaches, but it still involves discipline, support, focus, and accountability so I try not to get too distracted.

What does a typical work day look like for you?

A typical work day isn't always typical, that's what I love the most about working for myself.

My online business calendar is always organised with booking events and dates, plus the weekly plan in my trusted diary.

I prefer to know my plans for the week and then I decide which time and day is best to tackle them. Of course life and family events happen but the great advantage is that my days can be re-jigged about to suit my home and business life. I definitely work best later in the day, because usually I love being able to work on my cake creations without any interruptions.

How important has it been to have the right support and what impact has having that support had on your business and success?

Making little steps worked for me, such as meeting other like-minded mums in a business community 'who get it' in the brilliant Cocoon. I love meeting people, making new contacts, attending free business workshop events via the invaluable local Growth Hubs, and local business network events. They all build momentum and the belief in ourselves.

Following our gut feeling can sometimes create a series of events which involve meeting the right people just at the right time. A kind of 'stars are aligned' moment.

If you had your time again, is there anything you would do differently?

We all have fears that hold us back, and even after years of family life, work experience and following our passions, they still re-appear at times. Knowing what I know now is much better than what I thought I knew years ago. I now have a lot more self-confidence. If I had believed in myself much earlier on I think it would have helped me to grow that bit faster.

What's next for you?

My proudest moment recently has been winning two awards. After only eight months running my wedding cake business I was overwhelmed to win Regional South West and National Title at The Cake Professionals Awards 2020 for my Sea-themed cake design. These awards have given me an amazing confidence boost and the encouragement to just keep going.

Enjoying the now is so important, but creating new goals definitely keeps the momentum alive. I'm inspired by new trends and I am always on the lookout for new shiny objects (magpie habits).

Bonita's Top Tips:

1. Trust your gut instinct and do what is right for you, not to just to please others.

2. Stop regularly and smell those sweet roses, reward yourself and enjoy it too!

3. Ask for help and support from the right people or even better join a fabulous like-minded business group i.e The Mumpreneur Collective.

Key Takeaway

_____
_____
_____
_____
_____
_____
_____
_____
_____
_____

CORI JAVID

Business Name: Cori Javid Ltd
Website: www.corijavid.com

Cori Javid is a success coach, business mentor, host of The Limitless Mother Podcast and founder of The Limitless Mother Template Shop. She worked for an investment bank for 10+ years before deciding to create something more flexible, fulfilling and profitable for herself, and to empower other women to do the same. Cori believes that the world will be a better place when we get more money into the hands of women.

What did you do for a living before having children?

I worked in an investment bank as a trainer, mentor and coach but always felt a bit "lost" career wise, to be honest. I didn't feel particularly ambitious before I had my daughter and regularly used to think "there must be more to life than this" but felt totally at a loss as to what to do with my life.

Why did you decide to have a career change after becoming a mum?

I didn't at first! Returning to work after having my daughter was really hard. I didn't really want to go back at all but our financial situation then meant that I had no choice. Having fought tooth and nail to get a part-time (30 hours a week) arrangement, I felt like that was the best I could do. At the time, I felt well paid for part-time work and so I told myself, "this is as good gets". By that point I was managing teams and really struggled to make the whole work/life balance thing work. I felt miserable a lot of the time, wanting to be present with my daughter more (both mentally and physically) and consequently resentful but equally, I felt powerless to do anything about it.

The weird thing was, having my daughter had sparked ambition in me. Suddenly I had this little girl who was going to look up to me as her role model. I desperately wanted to do something with my life and feel like I was making a positive impact. But I had no idea what to do with that ambition. So I got promoted at work and immediately felt like I had been strapped into a train that I hadn't intended to board!

Then in the very same week that my daughter started school, the Universe evidently got fed up with my inaction and intervened. I found out I was being made redundant and felt as if the rug had been pulled from under me.

Turns out, that was one of the best things that has ever happened to me.

All of a sudden, I had choices. I could have tried to find a job elsewhere in the business, but I decided to take the severance package and run. I had no plan, just a fire in my belly.

I decided that it had to be possible to have it all: work that lights me up, a flexible schedule that allowed me to be the kind of mother I wanted to be; and money... really great money.

Did you struggle to make the transition to business owner?

Yes, but fortunately not for long. You see, there was a long lag between me finding out I was being made redundant and me actually leaving. During this time I started studying anything I could get my hands on around personal development and mindset. From there I got really into the Law of Attraction and money mindset and by the time I actually started my business I had cultivated a fairly solid mindset. One solid enough at least to realise that left to my own devices, I would likely self-sabotage by being paralysed by fear!

For a couple of months before I launched my business,

"I made the decision to bet on myself and believe in possibility, rather than to let fear call the shots"

I was consuming all the free content I could get my hands on, learning how to grow a business online. I was doing a lot of the behind-the-scenes work and I started coaching a couple of people for free. The problem was, I was taking no real action to get visible. I was afraid of what people would think and for some reason, in particular, my ex-colleagues.

I decided enough was enough and hired my coach (who I still work with to this day). Spending thousands of pounds on myself when we were in the middle of a massive structural renovation project on our house and while I had been out of work for months was certainly scary. But I made the decision to bet on myself and believe in possibility, rather than to let fear call the shots. That was another pivotal moment for me.

Within a couple of weeks, I launched my business and three months later I had replaced my corporate salary. Within seven months I had doubled it. My income has only continued to grow from there. My investment in myself paid off!

Was there a lightbulb moment or a turning point where it all "clicked" for you?

It was that moment when I invested in myself that something in me shifted. I was all in. And I haven't really looked back since. There have been more lightbulb moments since then, but I'll share a particularly poignant one here.

About a year ago, I found a journal entry that I had written in the month before I hired my coach. I made a declaration in there that I was going to earn six figures doing work that I loved, coaching clients, working to my own schedule from home. I had zero evidence at the time that this was possible.

But I made a decision that it was happening.

As I read back that journal entry (which described all sorts of other details like, having regular spa days, more family holidays etc) I had full body goosebumps at the realisation that ALL of it had come true.

I now refer to that as The Manifestation Tipping Point: the point at which you are so overwhelmed by the incredible changes you have made in your life that you can no longer deny how much power you have over your reality.

Knowing that I could make such huge changes in my life, to feel happier, work less, enjoy life more and earn considerably more money spurred me on to keep creating more and sharpened the focus of my mission to help other women feel similarly empowered.

What does success look like to you?

I'm going to be 100% honest here: I feel TOTALLY successful. I say that because, well, it's true, but also because I want other women to own their success and allow themselves to feel it.

My personal version of success is living a life I am obsessed with. Doing work that lights my soul on fire, enjoying the freedom to spend plenty of time with my daughter and plenty of time just for me. Having a life rich with experience. And feeling empowered to earn, spend, receive and have money.

Success isn't measured, it's felt. You never get "there", because if you try to measure success, once you reach a certain "success marker" you immediately turn your sights to the next one. There is no arriving. And the only way, in my opinion, to be successful, is to start feeling successful right now. Regardless of where you are.

How does your work/life balance look?

When I started my business I made a vow to work a maximum of 25 hours a week and I have never veered from that, although in fact, I often work less.

In school time, I work approximately five hours a day. I could work more, but I love my mornings which I spend at the gym or doing yoga, drinking tea and journaling or listening to inspiring audios. In the school holidays I typically work two days a week, unless we're going away.

But to me, work/life balance isn't only about the hours you work. Like success, it's about how you feel. Because you could work 15 hours but spend the rest of your waking hours worrying about your business. That's not balance.

To be honest, that feeling of balance is something that I continuously cultivate. I don't always get it perfect of course! But I am committed to leading a balanced life so it's something I work at to make sure it doesn't slip.

What does a typical work day look like for you?

My days are pretty structured and I like it that way because it actually gives me a ton of freedom. I start every single day with journaling to get my mindset on point (even on weekends!) and follow that up with audio affirmations. Only about 5 minutes for each but this has been so fundamental to keeping my head in the game. After that, I don't do the school run in the morning most of the time (my husband and daughter cycle together) so I take myself off to the gym.

When I get home I spend some time having a cup of tea, looking out at the garden and just thinking. Having time to just sit and think can feel hard to make for yourself but it is when I get all my insights and great ideas. I don't start work until around 10am typically, sometimes as late as 11am. I find I am more productive and just feel better when I have slower starts with space for my health and wellbeing.

I'll spend time either on creative focus work before lunch (e.g. written content) or project work because that's when my brain is most creative. I always take at least a half-hour proper lunch break, by which I mean I sit at the kitchen table and don't do anything business-related. Most of the time I watch something

"Selling is simply offering someone the opportunity for you to help them."

Cori Javid

> *"There is simply no way I would have experienced the fast success, the business growth, the fantastic money results I have – and enjoyed the ride – without support. "*

upbeat on Netflix :)

Then my afternoons are all about my 1:1 clients. I do calls on Tuesdays - Thursdays and Mondays and Fridays are reserved for recording my podcast and CEO time. I usually finish up my work before I collect my daughter from school but I do just quickly check in with my clients in the evening while she's getting ready for bed.

Other than that, it is rare I work in the evenings as I like to have plenty of downtime to rest and recuperate! Then the last part of my daily routine is listening to a guided meditation when I'm in bed as I like to use that time to be filling my brain with empowering thoughts and manifesting as I drift off to sleep :)

How important has it been to have the right support and what impact has having that support had on your business and success?

Having the right support has been absolutely critical. There is simply no way I would have experienced the fast success, the business growth, the fantastic money results I have – and enjoyed the ride – without support.

I have invested in support again and again and it has always paid me back manyfold. Trying to do it alone just sets you up to struggle. I think as mothers it can be really hard sometimes to admit we need support (I was that kind of mother who would turn down the offer of a babysitter when my daughter was small!). But as mothers and business owners, time is our most precious resource. So I see investing in support as a method to not only shortcut my way to success but also to buy back time. Time I get to spend either in my business doing the things that will actually move the needle for my business or time I can spend with my family.

If you had your time again, is there anything you would do differently?

Literally nothing. Don't misunderstand me, there have been ups and downs and things that felt challenging or disappointing along the way. But I understand that this is just part of being a business owner. I have learned from every single instance. And I made a vow a long time ago to be my own best friend and not beat myself up if something goes "wrong", a promise which has served me so well.

So I would keep everything exactly as it is, because I choose to trust the path.

What's next for you?

I want to keep pushing the boundaries of what seems possible in terms of earning more without working more, so I'm now working on scaling my business to seven figures.

To me, the exciting things about that goal are the ideal of making seven figures worth of impact (that's a lot of financially empowered mothers!) and how I'll need to grow as a business owner (and just as a woman in general) to get there.

Cori's Top Tips:

1. Invest in your mindset and heal your relationship with money. This has been a complete game changer for me.

2. Stop trying to do it alone, invest in support and surround yourself with positive people who are going places too.

3. Don't make results or numbers in your business mean something about you or your potential for success. If something didn't go well, it simply means there's more to learn.

Key Takeaway

_____

_____

_____

_____

_____

_____

_____

_____

ELIZABETH LUSTY

Business Name: Love2sing Ltd
Website: www.love2sing.co.uk

Elizabeth is a musician and founder
of both Vchoir, an online choir of over
100 singers who meet virtually and also
Love2sing choirs – a collection of large face to face
community groups in London.

What did you do for a living before having children?
I worked freelance as a Rockschool graded music examiner
and as a production coordinator for BBC Learning. I was also
a gigging vocalist and drummer in a variety of covers and
originals bands.

**Why did you decide to have a career change after
becoming a mum?**
I wanted to create a job that paid a full-time wage in part-time
hours, a flexible business where I could work from home and
choose when and how I worked. I wanted to be around for
my kids.

**Did you struggle to make the transition to
business owner?**
It might appear that, because I work in a creative industry, my
business is just a hobby. And in the beginning I spent a lot of
time giving too much and not paying myself. And I allowed
people to not take what I was doing seriously. For example, my
choirs run in terms, and when the term ended people would
often say things like "Oh lucky you, you get two weeks off
now!" But, the truth is, I spend that time learning new songs,

scheduling content, advertising, doing my accounts and a million other things.

I have and still do struggle with imposter syndrome. Even when I passed into my tenth year of profitable business, and was by then commanding a small team, I still did not feel comfortable putting a "10 Years" badge on my logo. I felt a fraud, and I continue to work on this. I struggle with perfectionism, and cling to the idea that if I plan every single detail and hold onto every aspect of control somehow I will prove my worth or get it right (whatever right is). In reality I have learned this causes stress and reduces my ability to lead, so now I try to live by the rule "Good is Good Enough!"

Was there a lightbulb moment or a turning point where it all "clicked" for you?

I felt I wanted to grow my business but I was unsure how to do that, so I joined The Cocoon online business club. As I started to learn and gain confidence, I felt more comfortable in sharing my struggles no matter how big or small. During a one-to-one session with Erin, she opened up the idea of outsourcing and allowing some of my control to fall on others. This changed my world and has continued to. After this session I sat down and wrote a list of all the tasks that I was doing myself. I was quite shocked. I hadn't quite realised that I was doing so much. It should have been obvious but until I saw it written down it didn't really hit me. I went onto The Cocoon and asked if anyone knew a VA (virtual assistant) who could help me. I found a wonderful life saver called Kelle from She's a Keeper. I went through my document and picked out things I felt comfortable handing over. At first that wasn't a lot. I wasn't used to letting go. Once the trust between us built up I started to add things.

As these things were taken away from me I started to be able to look at my business with fresh eyes. I started to have ideas again. I started to think about maybe taking on a new choir

"My mindset has changed and I now actively seek out people who are already doing things I would like to do."

leader to take over a choir that I no longer had time to run. I then thought I might try to open another choir. I learnt a lot from taking on my new leader and was able to use this to do a better job the second time round. I then realised that marketing and finding leaders took so much time it might be better to licence my business. So this is where I am today. I am in the middle of creating my licensee prospectus and one of my leaders has agreed to be my trial licensee!

What does success look like to you?

Success for me would be financial freedom and happy staff and customers. If the members of my choirs feel supported and valued my business will grow. If my staff feel supported and valued my business will be a success. Financial freedom for me would be in the form of a few fab holidays a year and shopping for groceries where I like and not where I feel I should to save pennies.

When I started my business my main goal was to earn the salary I had at my full-time job in the media but working part-time and being the boss. This seemed like an impossible task. Then the kids came along! I felt like maybe I had picked a ridiculous goal. I joined The Cocoon and quickly started to make connections with other inspiring women. It was really when I started outsourcing that things kicked off for me.

I was sceptical at first just thinking about how much I had to pay these people. Little did I know that freeing up this time would allow me to explore ideas I had kept under wraps. I slowly began to outsource more, and employ people. I had time

"*Don't be scared to make making money a priority. Making good money is nothing to be ashamed of.*"

Elizabeth Lusty

to systematise elements of my business making them slick and work like clockwork.

Then I started paying myself a salary. Something I just didn't believe would happen. Before, I had taken what I could, living on the edge each month, hoping I could make my contribution to the mortgage and bills, not wanting to feel ashamed and having to ask my partner to cover me... again.

In 2019 I realised I had done it – I had earned the full-time salary I had in my old job working 40 hours. I did this whilst working on average 3.5 days a week, plus I have three members of staff and my business is growing. My salary now equals and will soon surpass my husband's full-time wage. I pay myself a proper salary every month and it feels awesome.

How does your work/life balance look?

Pretty good. In some ways I think I am in a reasonably progressive situation. My partner does childcare Monday and Tuesday and I do it Wednesday – Friday with a little grandparent help when they can. When I don't have concerts or other events, I switch off my work phone on Friday afternoons and I don't turn it back on until I sit down at my desk on Mondays.

What does a typical day look like for you?

Working day: This means it is Daddy day – the kids know whatever they ask me I'm going to say "It's Daddy day – you need to ask Daddy". I get up first as soon as the chaos starts. I grab my brekky (I prepare it the night before), make a huge coffee, grab my phones and head to my office at the end of the garden. I usually have a list that I put together at the end of the last working day with the tasks that are most important. Then an A4 piece of paper with everything else I need to do i.e. order paper, get ink, email someone etc.

I try not to open my emails until I am two hours in because I just spend ages going through them and procrastinating.

I work solidly until 11.30 stop for lunch for 15 minutes then I head out to teach my choir.

I get home when school has finished and I spend 30 minutes with the kids and make another coffee (I like coffee). Back to the office. If I am not too busy my son comes down to my office for 30 minutes to do homework at my desk whilst I do emails. I write the list for the next day, switch off my work phone, put it in the drawer and head to the house.

How important has it been to have the right support and what impact has having that support had on your business and success?

One hundred per cent. This has been the catalyst for change for me as an individual. My mindset has changed and I now actively seek out people who are already doing things I would like to do. I ask for a conversation and I've found that they are more than happy to share their experiences and share their do's and don'ts. This is invaluable.

If you had your time again, is there anything you would do differently?

I would have asked for support sooner and outsourced some of the smaller business tasks. If you're taking your time answering basic enquiries and saving receipts to folders you cannot look at the bigger picture.

Once the Coronavirus lockdown hit in 2020 I had to turn my existing choirs into virtual choirs and learn about Zoom and all kinds of technology I hadn't worked with before. We decided we would record one hour's worth of teaching for our members, then meet up on Zoom for a face-to-face rehearsal. This was a success and we have managed to keep our choirs running.

But, I realised that there were lots of people out there without access to anything like this. I was surprised by how connected we all felt when we met on Zoom. I would be singing and playing the audio backings and the members were singing along at home (muted) but can see each other on screen. I decided I would like to run a group for everyone – no experience – no harmonies, just well known hits. I decided to open a virtual choir. I called it Vchoir.

I had outsourced my website build to a wonderful web designer, Caitlin Pieters, and she was in the process of building me a new site for another idea I had. We agreed that, for a small fee, she would turn this site into the new Vchoir site – we had it up and running in two weeks.

I used my contacts in The Cocoon to answer any techy questions about Mailchimp, Facebook and Zoom and I ran my first session to 192 people. It was so popular the following week I took on a leader who specialises in running choirs for the elderly and people with dementia and we called it the Silver Sing Along. That now runs every week and we have elderly couples, people living alone and all kinds of members singing with us. My working days now look very different. For the foreseeable future I will be using Facebook Live, Zoom and YouTube to share singing with as many people as I can. Going forward we hope to create a membership structure to Vchoir.

What's next for you?
I plan to license my business and grow my team nationally.

Elizabeth's Top Tips:

1. Contact other business owners and ask for advice.

2. Join The Cocoon.

3. Don't be scared to make making money a priority. Making good money is nothing to be ashamed of.

Key Takeaway

_____

_____

_____

_____

_____

_____

_____

_____

_____

_____

CLAIRE ADDISCOTT

Business Name: MIndful Sips and
Addiscotts Dog Food
Website: www.mindfulsips.co.uk

Claire is the founder of Mindful Sips.
She coaches women who are curious
about exploring their drinking habits to
make the connection between choice and being a
mindful drinker for better emotional wellbeing and
happiness. Since leaving the corporate world 13 years
ago she has built three other businesses around her
three children and her dogs.

What did you do for a living before having children?
My first role was in retail management and I spent a couple of
years there before realising it wasn't for me. I moved into the
corporate sector working for an airline's executive members'
club. Just over a year later I had my first little bundle of joy
at 22 years old, and 14 months after that, my second bundle
of joy.

I returned to work when my youngest was ten months old,
working for the Chairman and Chief Executive of the same
company. After the tragedy of 9-11, the industry changed.
Funding for projects was stopped so I decided to take my
experience to the charity sector as the Events Manager for a
small pregnancy charity working closely with midwives and
consultants. I absolutely loved it.

**Why did you decide to have a career change after
becoming a mum?**
In 2005 we decided to relocate the family from London to

Dorset and have bundle number 3. When she started school the time came to reignite my passion for work and try to reconnect my brain to the real world after nearly six years out. I went through all the usual channels but the truth was that after what I considered to be a relatively short time out, I was very out of touch with current practices. Technology had moved on and pretty much every prospective employer wanted proficiency in software I had little familiarity with. Then there were the problems of school hours, term time, hourly wages being less than the job I had left six years ago and childcare costs outweighing salary during the holidays and half terms.

I realised I had to work something out for myself. It needed to fit around our children and still allow me to be a good mum but it needed to challenge me too. Starting my own business seemed logical. I mean how hard can it be? (Oh how I laugh at my naivety now!!)

Did you struggle to make the transition to business owner?

I struggled because I had never started a business before and running a small 'one woman band' was very different to working in the corporate or charity sector with a team around me. I had no funds so I was doing everything myself, but this meant also doing an enormous amount of learning in the process. Time management was a real issue for me because I kept prioritising the children and letting things with the business drift. The more this continued the more I doubted my ability to run my business. I got extremely frustrated with my apparent inability to focus and the monkey mind of negative talk played a huge part in my struggle to succeed. Being behind in the tech world was also an issue... very steep learning curve!

Was there a lightbulb moment or a turning point where it all "clicked" for you?

My first lightbulb moment followed on from my frustrations

"*Join a community. It will be the biggest, most amazing and favourite business tool you will EVER have.*"

Claire Addiscott

#MumpreneurEvolution

with my second business Cakes and Cookies. I knew I was very good at what I did and often moved customers to tears, but there was a lot of time spent designing and quoting which were quite often met with comparisons to supermarket cake costs. It was demoralising and the time/cost/income ratios were awful. The real money was in wedding cakes and I just didn't have the confidence to step out of my comfort zone.

It was time to move on, but to what? We had welcomed a puppy, Delta, to the family. We soon discovered that she had tummy troubles and we had difficulties finding the right food to help her. Both my daughter and I are gluten intolerant so I had spent a lot of time reading and researching it, and it dawned on me that maybe that was Delta's problem too. I set to work looking for a manufacturer that would tick all my boxes for a high quality food for Delta and, as I did so, I realised if my dog was having this problem there was a strong likelihood that others were too. I closed down Cakes and Cookies to set up my third, and what I call my first 'proper', business!

I was still doing it all myself but I was able to stay at home with my dogs and children rather than going back to the workplace (if I had thought it was difficult before, it was even more complicated now we had two dogs). I felt sure this was the business I could make prosper. Connecting with dog lovers who had an interest in nutrition and wellbeing became my passion, and it encompassed the skills I had from my corporate and charity days as well as the learnings from my first two small business efforts. This was also the first time I invested in a business course to help me get things on the right track with processes and systems to help make it more efficient and scalable. I got my first business start-up loan!

My second lightbulb moment was when I realised I had a calling of a very different kind which, in a sense, brought learnings from my work and my personal life together in a life changing way. Addiscotts Dog Food was turning out to be pretty much a full-time job for very much part-time money!

I had won an award and been in the national press but I just didn't have the budget I needed to compete with the big boys in the industry and I couldn't match their discounts or offers. I was reinvesting all the profit to try to scale up the business and starting to question its viability. How much longer could I keep reinvesting my time and headspace into a project that seemed unable to step up a notch? I was caught in a Catch-22 spending loop of profit and investment, two years in and still in start-up debt.

I absolutely loved my relationship with my customers and their dogs, but was terrified I was about to hit a brick wall with business number 3. When do you draw the line and call it a day on a business you have truly poured your heart and soul into? How could I let those who believed in me down?

A small local event put things into perspective. I spoke to some lovely dog owners and cuddled lots of adorable dogs. I also had more new customers that day than from any other large event. I realised that my customers were loyal to my business because of me, because I had a passion, because I genuinely cared about them and their pooches. The answer was to scale back and treat it like the part-time business the money was dictating it was. But that meant I needed another source of income. I had heard a lot about membership sites and passive income and was already dabbling with the idea of starting a subscription service for dog food, courses on dog nutrition and holistic wellbeing.

Meanwhile, in my personal life, my health had been gradually declining, nothing life-threatening, just unexplained niggles and pains. I was a party girl and loved to drink and celebrate any occasion, with or without friends! Drinking had become a habit and weekend binge drinking a regular occurrence. Long story short, one morning I decided to cut out alcohol and take a break from the booze. I was looking for a helping hand and some support along the way with some hints and tips to help me succeed, but I wanted it to be mostly holistic.

I discovered that there was help available with cutting alcohol

---

I absolutely loved my relationship with my customers and their dogs, but was terrified I was about to hit a brick wall with business number three.

---

out of my life forever, but not much support for people who simply wanted assistance with moderating their drinking. Once again it dawned on me that if I had this problem, there must be others that needed a solution too. Short courses and a membership would be the ideal way to facilitate that, whilst also supplementing the income from the business I already had. Mindful Sips is a true culmination of everything I learned in my previous three businesses, going back to my roots of project work and teaching but encompassing my passion for holistic health and well-being. All those personal and professional paths have come together and intertwined to create a business that I believe can help impact peoples' lives in a positive way.

What does success look like to you?

I have felt an element of success with all my businesses. The drive to get my first business off the ground lead me to learn. Did I feel like a failure when I made the decision to walk away from it and do something else? Yes of course I did, and there was a lot of reflection about the mistakes I made, but ultimately it was a success because it moved me back into the working world and got my brain thinking differently. Cakes and Cookies helped me drag what I learnt about balancing customer expectations and what made good business sense from the depths of my brain. It made me realise everything I love about the different walks of life and human nature. When I decided the business was no longer serving me, I was so disappointed in myself for not being stronger, for not having "what it takes" to be a success. But the truth is, it was never going to be a success as it wasn't right for us. I had to realise that and see it for what it really was – a stop gap.

Addiscotts dog food is a success. It has taught me to separate business and my personal life. To put clear boundaries in place, to manage customer expectations better, to automate as much as possible and put systems in place. It might not be a success on the scale I had hoped it would be, but it is the business that has made me a business woman.

Mindful Sips is already a success and there is so much still to discover. My learnings from it are so powerful: it is teaching me to trust in those around me; to learn from others; to know that I don't have to do it all myself, and to enjoy the clarity to be gained from other people's knowledge.

How does your work/life balance look?

Work-life balance is a balancing act in itself. As a Libra, I really strive for perfect balance in my life, but I've never found the perfect combination, and as our children have grown and changed, so have the family dynamics. We've gone from set bedtimes to clubs that mean late nights; from having dependent children that need constant ferrying, to the boys becoming independent and driving themselves. From working school hours, to squeezing in extra time in the evening while I wait for one of the boys to come home. From gym memberships in a bid to stay committed to self-care, to yoga videos in the lounge

My learnings from it are so powerful: it is teaching me to trust in those around me; to learn from others; to know that I don't have to do it all myself, and to enjoy the clarity to be gained from other people's knowledge.

because income was tight for a while. I feel our family work/life balance is always changing. We get it figured out for a time, and then we need to adjust again. As with any normal family unit, that has its ups and downs, sometimes it's a struggle, sometimes it's a breeze. But as a team we're always adaptable and I think that is the best work/life balance you can ask for.

How important has it been to have the right support and what impact has having that support had on your business and success?

I think having the right support is fundamental to business success. I spent the first year of Addiscotts trying to do it myself, reading books and signing up for every freebie. Getting a start-up loan and investing in a business academy gave me the commitment to make it work and keep up the momentum. Whilst the business isn't what I thought it would be, the mentoring and coaching gave me the courage to explore, overcome uncertainty and find clarity I needed to keep the business alive, rather than just throwing in the towel and feeling like I had failed again.

When I started Mindful Sips, investing in The Cocoon was one of the first things I did. I had learned my lesson. The Cocoon has been a support on another level too because, for me, the fact that it has local events has had a huge impact. I've made some incredible business friends and have a community of other business mums to turn to. Going to events and seeing familiar faces to laugh with, being able to meet up to run through ideas and talk face to face is invaluable. Even though it is an international membership and is mostly online, it has the feel of a tight knit community. Having support is really important to your growth and development. Having the right support is what helps make you a success.

Every business has taught me something, both about the business industry and more importantly, about myself!

If you had your time again, is there anything you would do differently?

No, I don't think so. No matter how frustrating, sad or disappointing it might be at the time, I can look back and see a clear path of learning. Every business has taught me something, both about the business industry and more importantly, about myself!

What's next for you?

I've found my passion. My experiences have given me what it takes to carry this business forward, for it to challenge me enough to feed my soul and enough space for it to grow as I do. Next stop… a book! "Alcohol and Me: A mindfully written account"… or something similar!

Claire's Top Tips:

1. It's OK to change your mind. The business that works for you today might not work for you tomorrow. But nothing is wasted. You either win or you learn. Never give up!

2. Don't sweat the small stuff. Take the time to look after and be with those you love. We chose to be entrepreneurs so we have that freedom after all. It will all still be there tomorrow and your business WILL NOT collapse because you didn't put a post on social media for a week!

3. Join a community. It will be the biggest, most amazing and favourite business tool you will EVER have.

Key Takeaway

_____

_____

_____

_____

_____

_____

LOUISE GATES

Business Name: Gates Digital Consultancy
Website: www.gatesdigitalconsultancy.com

Louise works with women who are
feeling frustrated or overwhelmed when
using Search and Social Media Marketing
for their business. She supports them with
outsourced Done-For-You packages and One-To-One
Training, with an emphasis on Advertising, so they can
confidently make more money without giving up more
of their time, and spend it with their loved ones instead.

What did you do for a living before having children?

I've worked in Digital Marketing my whole career – 15 years
and counting! The majority of that time was gaining valuable
experience at media agencies, but before I had my son I was working
at Sky as the lead digital strategist for a new product launch.

Why did you decide to have a career change after becoming a mum?

On maternity leave I met many inspirational women who
had created businesses from a passion that worked around
their families and lifestyles. However, quite a few of them
were struggling with marketing their businesses because it was
something they had never done before. At the same time, I felt
there wasn't enough flexibility with my corporate role alongside
my new role as mum.

I wanted to help the women I met on maternity leave and
was craving more flexibility for my own new family... so
Gates Digital Consultancy was born! After becoming a mum,
I wanted to spend as much time as I could with my son, but

131

I hadn't lost my ambition and I felt driven to show him there isn't just one way to be successful. You can have an idea, feel a fire in your belly, and go for it!

Did you struggle to make the transition to business owner?

It was the best decision I could have made and I love what I do, but it hasn't been easy. Lots of beliefs and mindset limitations come up that you never realise you had, and you have to deal with them to keep moving forward. For example, I discovered I had a fear of failure as well as fear of success... yes really! It meant I stayed stuck for a while not taking the steps I needed to in order to grow my business. Financially, the transition was a bit of a struggle as well. I went from being an equal earner in our household to bringing in less than a quarter of my corporate salary. We had to tighten the purse strings and were much more cautious about spending money. However, it did make us better at managing our finances and pushed us to make some smart financial decisions.

In the beginning, I struggled to find a flexible balance between work and family and often felt guilty for spending time on either one. There was no quick fix here and what worked for me might not work for you, you just have to test different things and find out what suits you best. When the guilt crept up, it helped to remind myself of my core values and why I started my business. This removed some of the overwhelm and helped me to re-focus.

Was there a lightbulb moment or a turning point where it all "clicked" for you?

When I became crystal clear on who I wanted to work with and what services I wanted to offer them, things began to really pick up. I started getting more consistent leads and I was converting them into clients.

I'd gone through a long period of getting little to no leads and being told I was too expensive. I was feeling negative, really frustrated, and embarrassed that I was struggling while all around me I could see people celebrating wins. I wondered whether I should go back to a corporate role, but when I heard the saying "What you think you are, you are", I realised that things weren't going to change unless I did. I started taking myself and my mindset more seriously, hired a coach, invested in training and changed some of my processes.

There was no single action that increased my leads, rather an accumulation of several things. I took lots of consistent actions to increase my visibility and share my knowledge with my ideal clients, and I pushed myself out of my comfort zone a lot. My marketing resonated with people more as I became clearer about who I was talking to. I didn't see results immediately however, so I advise others to stay the course and have faith that you're doing the right thing.

I started converting leads into clients when I reminded myself that rather than selling my services, I was using my expertise to help someone solve a problem. If I didn't think I could assist someone the way they needed it, I was honest and said so. I think this genuine desire to help people shone through and helped me to really connect with my ideal clients.

What does success look like to you?

To me, success is a lifestyle of choice. I'd love to create a lifestyle for my family that isn't restricted by money worries – enjoying lovely family holidays, weekend trips with my husband, exploring hobbies with the kids, and saving for their future. My greatest lifestyle goal for my family is to enable my husband to work closer to home because he currently works away during the week.

I do feel some success now in creating a rewarding balance between work and family. I've been able to spend lots of time with my son and also have clear dedicated business time.

How does your work/life balance look?

Until recently, I worked three days a week while my son went to preschool, giving me two whole days to spend with him by myself each week. With a baby girl now in tow this scenario will take a different shape, but I'm determined to find something that works for all of us again.

I create regular opportunities to work on my own business alongside my clients' businesses. It's so easy to let your own marketing drop when you're looking after others, but it's important to keep taking those consistent actions.

I like to create clear boundaries around work and family time so that everyone's expectations are met. Sometimes this means I work in the evenings to catch up, but as a rule I keep them free to have some down-time and re-energise for the next day.

What does a typical work day look like for you?

I tried many things before I found a routine that worked well for me, and with an additional family member this will need to be adapted again, however the following worked for me...

I would wake up before my son most mornings to complete my most important tasks (when my brain works best), and implement self-development post-lunch to motivate myself for the afternoon (when my brain works less well). Working by yourself means you rely less on others to stay motivated and focussed, so understanding when I worked best was essential.

Post pre-school drop-off I usually scheduled client calls so

"This year I also made a concerted effort to meet people online and in-person who do the same thing as I do. I love working for myself but miss having colleagues. This has led to some fantastic connections!

I could action relevant tasks during the day, and engaged in social media conversations on behalf of my business. I would then complete my most important tasks if I hadn't done so earlier.

Prior to pre-school pick-up I had a clear cut off point half an hour before I needed to leave the house to switch my brain back into "mum mode" to avoid bringing any stresses into my time with him.

How important has it been to have the right support and what impact has having that support had on your business and success?

I don't think I could have made the progress I have without my support. Knowing I have my family's support is invaluable, and my friends are great at reminding me of how far I've come when I'm having a down day.

This year I invested in a coach who I meet with monthly. She has been amazing. We've worked on my mindset together and talked through my plans and goals, and of course she has held me accountable! Having someone who knows my business inside out and wants me to succeed as much as I do has been more beneficial than I could have imagined.

This year I also made a concerted effort to meet people online and in-person who do the same thing as I do. I love working for myself but miss having colleagues. This has led to some fantastic connections! There's been the odd referral from this, but support and friendship has been at the forefront.

Lastly, it's impossible to know everything you need to know to grow a business, so asking for help and seeking advice from others has been really important. Joining The Cocoon opened me up to an incredible network of women who are skilled experts in their fields and willing to share their knowledge. They also feel like colleagues and it's a wonderful team to feel part of.

If you had your time again, is there anything you would do differently?

I'd have invested in the above earlier on and given myself a break from the guilt! In all honesty, I think you need to learn the lessons to progress and grow. I'm where I am meant to be right now and I will achieve my goals if I keep learning and moving forward.

What's next for you?

My next challenge is to create a balance of work and family with a new baby daughter. I'll take a step back for a short while to spend time adjusting to having two small children – while I'm confident my clients are being looked after well by a fantastic connection I made.

Long term, I want to keep helping women-owned small businesses feel less frustrated and overwhelmed when using social media on a one-to-one basis, but I also plan to launch new products that aim to help my ideal clients improve their social media marketing for themselves. I'm developing an online program in a way that I don't believe has been created before which really excites me! I also plan to create e-guides that provide practical steps that address specific problem areas I know my clients struggle with. I can't wait!

Louise's Top Tips

1. Surround yourself with a support network that inspires and teaches you.

2. Invest in yourself – time or money – to keep growing as a person and a business.

3. There is no one-size-fits-all for success so take lots of consistent actions and find what works for you.

Key Takeaway

_____

_____

_____

_____

_____

_____

_____

_____

_____

_____

LAURA ROBINSON

Business Name: Worditude Ltd
Website: www.worditude.co.uk

Laura is a copywriting coach for
small business owners who write
their own online content. She runs
her business while home-schooling
her teenage sons, and has a growing collection of
business, marketing and copywriting qualifications
because she can never resist the chance to earn a
certificate. Laura likes drinking gin, paddling at the
beach, and watching Formula 1 racing (not all at
the same time).

What did you do for a living before having children?
I went straight from university to a graduate program in
a financial services company, where I worked mostly in
Communications and Marketing roles. By 23 I was married,
had a middle management position, and was expecting my first
child. I have no idea why I was in such a hurry – I've always
taken life at that pace.

Why did you decide to have a career change after becoming a mum?
I had no intention of giving up my job. I'd planned to have
two children close together in age, return to work full-time, and
hurtle up the career ladder.

Son #2 was born with a compromised immune system (he
has completely recovered now) which meant for the first few
years we were in and out of hospital for appointments and
emergency admissions. It also meant he couldn't be left in a

childcare facility. So my husband and I both went part-time so we could share the family duties.

Over the next two years, alongside my son's health problems, I had a burst appendix, my Mum was diagnosed with breast cancer (now recovered), her mother died from the same disease, my husband was made redundant… and then the day before Christmas Eve I contracted pleurisy. In the New Year (2009) I went back to work, but I was mentally broken, and in March that year I walked out on my job, literally – I just didn't go back one day.

I know that's a long back story, but I share it because it didn't take courage to quit work and start my own business. I really didn't feel like I had a choice, because I couldn't cope with having a job any longer. That pressure has kept me going. There have been plenty of times when having a job looked like an easier option, but there was no way I was going to go back to employment.

Did you struggle to make the transition to business owner?

YES! I freelanced as a content writer for web design agencies for a few years, and even though I was based at home, I was very much in an employee mentality. They dealt with the clients, they just told me what to do and I got on with it.

I was so ineffective with my time – I would fill six hours every day because I felt like I should be working all the time the boys were in school. I had no plan for how to increase my income, or make my work more satisfying.

Initially, we took a big drop in income as I was the main earner, and my husband had worked part-time.

He went back to full-time work, but we were still living in our overdraft most of the time. Our children were young so they didn't ask for expensive things, and I doubt I would've been brave enough to take them on holiday anyway. By the time they were old enough to appreciate days out and holidays, we were able to manage an annual pilgrimage to Legoland and a short break at Centre Parcs. But we don't feel like we missed out.

Most of our family memories have been made doing the everyday stuff, like taking advantage of a sunny winter's day and heading to the local nature reserve. And we go to the beach almost every day in the Summer. We have a lot more time freedom, which means I don't feel the pressure to spend money.

Was there a lightbulb moment or a turning point where it all "clicked" for you?

I had a run of very boring website-content jobs. They were so dull. And I realized I just couldn't face having no control over the work anymore. Around the same time I invested in a qualification with the Institute of Data & Marketing (IDM) which helped me feel more credible, even though I already had a business degree. That's when I decided to set up my own website, and register as a Limited Company.

What does success look like to you?

When I first left my job, my boys were only two and four. I knew that by the time they were both in secondary school I'd really be feeling the pressure (from family, husband and maybe even myself) to go back to work, but I didn't want the boys to come home every afternoon to an empty house. So I set myself the challenge to be earning enough by then that it would make

"I feel so happy that we've been able to do this. It is 100% the right thing for our family, and having this option feels like success to me."

financial as well as practical sense for me to stay self-employed.

Between then and now Son #2 has been diagnosed with autism, and Son #1 has had his own difficulties with school and mental health, and we decided to take them both out of the school system to home educate them. This is only possible because I work for myself.

I feel so happy that we've been able to do this. It is 100% the right thing for our family, and having this option feels like success to me.

How does your work/life balance look?

Ha ha ha ha ha ha ha ha ha

No seriously, pass me the gin.

You know how a tightrope walker never really looks stable? They must have a very good sense of balance to do what they're doing, but to the onlooker it seems a bit wibbly-wobbly.

That's my life.

But it works for us.

I'm with the boys until 2pm every weekday. This is also when I get to see friends (at home-ed meet-ups), exercise (when we go for walks, or swimming), relax (in the woods, at the beach), watch TV (we love a good documentary or true-story film). Then in the afternoon and evenings I work. And I work for most of the weekend too.

What does a typical work day look like for you?

A typical week day…

• Wake up, have a coffee and quiet time, maybe journal.
• Housework
• Get the boys up, fed, dressed and ready for the day - they're 12 and 14 so not exactly babies but they need quite a bit of encouragement.
• 10-2pm is Home Ed time – we might go out and meet with friends, get outside, do maths on an online platform, watch a documentary, play board games.

- 2pm – 6pm is working time. I might have a client call.
- Each day has its own focus. Monday is for a retainer client. Tuesday is to focus on my own marketing. Wednesday is for 1-1 clients. Thursday and Friday are for my membership.

If I have a bigger client project on the go (copywriting for a complete sales funnel, or a total website rewrite), I'll work one day at the weekend.

How important has it been to have the right support and what impact has having that support had on your business and success?

This would not be possible without the support from online friends who are also building their own businesses. Every time I've freaked out about the viability of this... will I ever make enough money, will I recover that website I've just accidentally deleted, is everybody smiling at me while really thinking I'm a total idiot? My husband has been right there next to me, 100% freaking out too, so he's not been much help when it comes to support, even if he would like to be and means well. That's why I need my online friends and community. I've leaned on my online friends, learnt from them, celebrated with them.

I've benefited from being in large communities, group programs and having 1-1 coaching – whatever I could afford and/or needed at the time.

If you had your time again, is there anything you would do differently?

Start paying for things earlier. I squeaked by on the free version of everything for so long. I had such low self-confidence that I couldn't justify spending any money on myself – even if it was to help me earn more money.

What's next for you?

Over the last few months I've nudged my business away from copywriting and am focusing on coaching other business owners to improve their own copywriting. I love helping people communicate with their audience. It means I've got fewer products and services to sell, and I've simplified my marketing process too, so I can settle into a more manageable, predictable work routine.

Laura's Top Tips:

1. Set small goals and celebrate when you get there – the journey is made easier if you are travelling from one win to the next.

2. Know who can give you the support you need – it isn't always going to be your friends and family. They love you but they're probably also a bit freaked out by this unconventional life you've chosen.

3. Give yourself a budget to spend on business essentials from the beginning.

Key Takeaway

_____

_____

_____

_____

_____

_____

MAIJA PYKETT

Business name: Smallprint and
Silver Pet Prints
Websites: www.smallprint.com:
www.memory-treasures.com
www.silverpetprints.com

Maija had a career in publishing before she came
up with the idea of Smallprint, a jewellery business
making silver jewellery capturing children's
fingerprints, hand and footprints. Smallprint grew
quickly and eventually Maija decided that franchising
was the best way to offer her personalised jewellery
to a wider audience. She has since created a sister
brand to Smallprint called Memory Treasures, which
makes keepsakes for those who have lost a loved one.
She has also created a separate business called Silver
Pet Prints which captures pet's paws in silver.

What did you do for a living before having children?

I spent the first 15 years of my career working on the London
publishing scene as a writer, sub-editor and layout designer.
I worked on a wide variety of magazines, from consumer titles
such as House Beautiful and Good Housekeeping, through to
business magazines such as Marketing Week and Accountancy
Age. When I was pregnant with my first son, my husband and
I moved from London to Bristol.

Why did you decide to have a career change after becoming a mum?

I went back to work after my first son was born, but it was
tough. I always felt guilty when I had to stay off work if my

son was sick and the pressure to leave on time to pick him up from nursery caused tension too. My final job was on a local newspaper which was very 'old school' and frankly sexist. I was signed off with stress during my second pregnancy because my male boss was passing me over simply because I was pregnant. The final straw came when one by one he called each member of the editorial team into his office for a review and pay rise. When I asked why I had not been called in too, I was told it was 'because you are going on maternity leave'! I decided there and then that I would be handing in my notice after my maternity leave. The only slight snag was that I had absolutely no idea what I was going to do!

Did you struggle to make the transition to business owner?

When I started out, I didn't really think of myself as a business owner. I was so passionate about my idea, I didn't stop to think about the implications. Yes it was hard work, but I was carried forward on a tide of excitement and enthusiasm. What's more, my goal was simply to earn enough money so my children could go to nursery.

Was there a lightbulb moment or a turning point where it all "clicked" for you?

My eureka moment for the business came when Noah was three months old and it couldn't have fitted in with working around children more perfectly. When my eldest son Dylan was one and a half, I had been introduced to an amazing product called precious metal clay (soft to the touch in its raw state, but sterling silver once fired in a kiln). Having never come across anything like it before, I rolled out a piece and pressed Dylan's finger into it. It left a lovely little indent and some fingerprint lines too, but other than that it was very rustic! But I loved it because once it was fired, I had a silver pendant with a little dent that I knew had been put there by my son. I wore it every day.

A year or so later I had my second son Noah. When he was three months old, I took him to have his hand and footprints taken in clay and framed. As I stood in the queue of women waiting to have their babies' prints taken, I fingered my necklace and an idea began to form. While I will always treasure Dylan and Noah's clay hand and footprints, I loved my necklace even more because it could be with me all of the time. I began to ask myself if all these new mums might feel the same – whether I could come up with a range of jewellery featuring children's fingerprints. I ran it past my husband when he got home from work and he was enthusiastic. The next day I told a friend about my idea and she was blown away! When I saw her reaction I realised I had to give it a go.

It took me six long months between the germination of an idea to launch day. Every time Noah's eyes closed, I was on it! First and foremost I had to learn how to make the jewellery, no mean feat in itself when your background is in publishing! I took a couple of jewellery making courses and the rest was trial and error. Then I had to develop a range that included pendants, charms, cufflinks and key rings – in other words, something for all members of the family. I came up with the company name, Smallprint, and the logo, which I had created from my writing when I was about seven years old.

Next I had to think about photography, flyers and a website, for which my background in publishing proved really useful. Finally I had to source necklaces and bracelets to attach my jewellery to.

As for marketing, I did none! I didn't really know what marketing was and it simply didn't occur to me. Social media was only just emerging and was a long way from being the amazing marketing tool it is now, and I had no money to spend on advertising. But I did manage to get an article in the paper I used to work on a couple of months after launching, the quid pro quo being that I modelled for an article they ran on 'magic knickers'! That's dedication!

The first year was a whirlwind, a steep learning curve and a huge success.

So launch day arrived. I set up a stand in a large local baby store and stood there quietly quaking in my boots! I had never sold anything in my life and there I was with a completely new product, having done no marketing whatsoever!

The first person ventured up to my stand to admire my pieces. When I explained what it was, she whipped her purse out of her bag and said 'Right, what do I need to do?' While I was taking her toddler's fingerprints, more people ventured over and listened while I explained to the mum what I was doing and gradually a queue began to form. I didn't have time to be nervous. I just talked, took prints solidly for four hours and gave out a flyer to everyone who approached my stand (finally some marketing!)

In the first three months of launching I turned over three-quarters of my previous salary in publishing. I made a few mistakes to begin with in terms of production, but I bent over backwards to put those mistakes right, which often resulted in a further sale to the same customer.

The first year was a whirlwind, a steep learning curve and a huge success. There was no room for uncertainty or self-doubt and frankly the appetite for my jewellery spoke for itself. I loved every minute of it – meeting customers, taking prints and then making the jewellery at home.

The self-doubt came after that first year, when my business took a turn in a direction I had simply never anticipated. I received a call from Newcastle from a new mum who had heard about my jewellery from her sister who lived in Bristol. She wanted a piece made, but there was a slight snag... I needed her baby to take a print! I let her down gently and carried on with my business in Bristol. Then two friends, one from London and one who was moving to Australia, asked if I would teach them and set them up with Smallprint. I gave it some thought and decided I would give it a go. I had to be mindful of the fact that I was spending their money on all tools and materials and had to make sure I bought them only what they needed. I also had to devise a training course and written instructions.

Almost a year to the day of my own launch, two more Smallprint businesses started up, one in Sydney and one in South London. Both experienced the same success as I did, which was both a relief and a triumph.

Soon after, customers began to ask if I was part of a franchise and another germ of an idea began to form. At the time Smallprint only made fingerprint items and I needed access to the children in order to take the print. I didn't know much about franchising, but it began to look like a viable option for such a personalised business, not least because it meant other mums could enjoy the experience of working part-time while looking after their little ones.

I consulted the lawyer for the British Franchise Association and began to work towards putting together a model that would work as a franchise. The first time I put a sign up at the National Baby Show at the NEC saying I had a business opportunity on offer, I had nearly 50 enquiries!

And here is when the doubt began to creep in. Setting everything up, from the legal documents and Operations Manual to devising a more formal training course and equipment package, suddenly seemed overwhelming. I hadn't even signed up one franchisee and I was scared. I mentioned it to my husband the day before we came back from a holiday. There was a slight pause and then he said "Why don't I give up my job?"

To be clear, he was the main breadwinner working as Marketing Director for a prestigious law firm, and I had yet to sign up one franchisee. But his first day back at work he handed in his notice, we drafted a business plan for a loan over a cheeky Nandos! We were nervous, but we were very, very excited.

That was 2006, the year we launched our first eight UK franchises. Fourteen years on and we have 95 franchisees in 20 different countries. We have expanded our range to include hand and footprints as well drawings and writing. We have launched a sister brand to Smallprint called Memory Treasures which makes keepsakes for people who have lost a loved one and work with a number of children's charities and neo-natal wards that support parents who have lost a child. We have also launched a separate franchise called Silver Pet Prints which makes keepsakes with the owner's fur baby's paw print in miniature and which has also proved extremely popular.

What does success look like to you?

Success is hard to define for most small business owners because their business and the world in which we live changes every day. And while for some, success means making lots of money, for my husband and I, the time and devotion we put into our business is often as much a labour of love as it is means to earning our keep. We have always been there for the children without having to make excuses to anyone, which is probably what motivates many women who launch their own businesses.

For me personally the Memory Treasures brand is something I am extremely proud of. It never occurred to me that this was one of the routes we would take until I received a call one day from a lady whose friend had just lost her six month old baby. She asked if there was anything I could do and of course I said 'yes' immediately. I made her a beautiful pendant with her baby's fingerprint and the joy with which it was received was overwhelming. I couldn't bring myself to charge for it, thinking it would be a one off, but gradually that side of the business grew. And yes, it can be sad and emotional, but the privilege of making something that will give some small comfort to someone who has lost a loved one, cannot be measured in any terms. But I know I speak for our franchisees in saying that it is the most precious part of their business.

How does your work/life balance look?

Work/life balance? That's a tough one from a franchisor's perspective, because we are never off-duty. We have franchisees around the world, so emails are coming in 24 hours a day and we are dedicated to being there to support our franchisees when they need us. Yes, we are able to take extended summer holidays, but we always have to work while we are away which can sometimes be frustrating.

I think our franchisees would acknowledge that for them, the balance works well. There are enormously busy times of the year, Christmas being the big one, but then they can switch off and savour time with their families, while the back end of their business that is run by head office keeps ticking along. Our franchisees enjoy a flexible business that allows them to set the days they work and, in terms of making jewellery, that can be done in the evenings or when the children are having a nap.

What does a typical work day look like for you?

One of the things I love about running my own business is that there is no such thing as a 'typical' day. Running a Smallprint or Silver Pet Print business is definitely not a desk job. Every day is different, depending on the time of the year, whether you have an event that day, whether you are going to focus on marketing or manufacturing. And because our franchise is deliberately a flexible one, the aim is that most of what a franchisee does can fit in around the family.

All marketing and manufacturing is done at home, so I would allot a time in the day when the children were at nursery or school, or in the evening once they have gone to bed. Events can vary in themselves from taking prints in a customer's home, to holding print sessions in shops or at baby shows, craft shows or Christmas fairs.

If I have an event, the day would begin by making sure I have everything I need gathered together and enough supplies of materials. The events themselves are great fun because you meet so many interesting people, old and young, so there's never a dull moment.

Pet shows can also be interesting! All of our Silver Pet Print franchisees are passionate about animals, so getting to chat to pet owners and meet their fur babies… well, what's not to love!

How important has it been to have the right support?

I think support is vital, and there wasn't much around when I started out! As a small business owner, you can't expect to know everything. And as a mum who owns a small business, that support is even more important because you are juggling lots of balls. Smallprint and Silver Pet Print franchisees benefit from on-going support from head office (it's one of the main reasons people become part of a franchise network) and they know they have a much better chance of succeeding with the support of an already-successful brand, its head office and their fellow franchisees.

For those mums starting out in business on their own, The Cocoon membership is an absolute must. The sheer volume of shared knowledge that it offers is invaluable. But equally important is being part of a group of women who are all striving for the same goals – to make a success of their business while still being able to bring up a family.

It is easy to get caught in the trap of thinking you can master everything on your own and that simply isn't possible unless you are Wonder Woman! Being part of a group who actively share their knowledge and expertise is priceless. And what's more, you have access to tools that will give you a head start – and as a working mum, who doesn't need that?. The Mumpreneur Collective is exactly that – a collective of women supporting each other in their business endeavours.

If you had your time again, is there anything you would do differently?

I honestly don't think I would do anything differently if I had my time again. That doesn't mean I haven't made mistakes, but you can't anticipate every single eventuality and you are always going to make mistakes. The crucial point is you learn from them. Few mistakes are catastrophic, and making small mistakes in business will hopefully enable you to avoid making potentially bigger ones down the line.

What's next for you?

I continue to grow and develop our businesses. Times have changed and we have to change with the times. It is easy to think that because something is working you can just carry on doing the same thing, but you can't. Eventually a marketing technique, a social media platform or a product grows stale. If you want to stay ahead of the game, you have to be adaptable and open to change.

I am also learning more traditional silversmith techniques and have recently launched a business called Carnelian Bay which sells contemporary jewellery made by me.

Maija's Top Tips:

1. Be realistic about how much time you have to spend on your business and stick to it.

2. Don't be afraid to reach out and ask for help and support, you are going to need it.

3. Celebrate your successes and learn from your failures, then move on!

Key Takeaway

_____

_____

_____

_____

_____

_____

_____

_____

_____

NICOLE GABRIEL

Business Name: The Work
Psychologist/Serene Mind/
Hugged by Nature
Website: www.serenemind.co.uk

Nicole is a qualified psychologist.
She considered self-employment prior to having
children, but becoming a parent was the catalyst for
making the change. Since making the move to self-
employment she has focused on creating a portfolio
of work rather than 'a business', which includes working
as an associate diversity and inclusion consultant, a
freelance coaching psychologist and a jewellery maker.

What did you do for a living before having children?
I worked as an HR Manager/HR Business Partner in
various corporate settings, including Financial Services and
the Police.

**Why did you decide to have a career change after
becoming a mum?**
Self-employment was something I had been thinking about
anyway, although I did actually go back to a corporate HR
Manager role after having my son. He was four years old when
I eventually cut the ties! It was the struggle of trying to juggle
the demands of being a professional in a corporate setting with
the demands of parenthood that gave me the courage to walk
away. I wanted to be 'present' for my son (and my husband),
not just physically, but emotionally too and the lack of time
freedom and the emotional drain of my job meant that it no
longer worked for me.

Did you struggle to make the transition to business owner?

It has taken me some time to get to the right place in my head. One of the difficulties I had is that I did not see myself as a 'business owner'. I just knew that I wanted to be in control of my own time so that I could be the parent I wanted to be. The journey has been one of a steep learning curve, not just about how to run a business (which I knew NOTHING about prior to diving in!) but also about myself. So, I have definitely had to face, head-on, fears about not being good enough, about being judged, about it not working out, about not making enough money, as well as having to work hard at my perfectionist tendencies and trying not to compare myself with other people doing similar things. I have also had the pressure from family about giving up a 'good' job and the financial impact that has had – especially as it has taken me a while to find the path I want to give my energy to. Giving myself permission to be me, after years of fitting a corporate mould, has been quite challenging. The path has involved lots of reading and personal discovery accompanied by various kinds of training, false starts and much exploration and experimentation. Seven years later I think I'm about there.

Was there a lightbulb moment or a turning point where it all "clicked" for you?

I don't feel that I've had one big lightbulb moment, more a series of small ones creating a string of lights! A couple of

---

The journey has been one of a steep learning curve, not just about how to run a business ... but also about myself.

---

years ago I spent a morning doing a Vision Board. I think that consolidated for me all the different things that I'd encountered on my path into one clear place, and that has been hugely helpful ever since in allowing me to stay more centred on my values and my overall goal for my working life. I now feel much more aware of when I am veering off-course, and much more aware of when I am focusing on the right things.

A second 'ping' was overcoming my block of not starting anything because I wasn't ready. I understood that until I start doing something new I'm never going to get better at it, but truly believing that and actually taking the plunge and facing my fear of failure, the perfectionism associated with that, and my lack of self compassion (which I am also getting better at) has been a huge leap forward. I put this into practice when I agreed to have a stall at a local Art and Craft fair to sell my jewellery that I'd been talking about doing for years! I received a lot of positive feedback about it, and sold a few pieces, which made me feel thoroughly energised

What does success look like to you?

Success for me is doing a job I love and feel proud of, that energises me, earns a healthy living and enables me to maintain positive wellbeing and be my best self with my family (more of the time anyway!!). The financial aspect is easier to measure, and I'm not quite there yet, but as for the rest, I know that it's working when I am not stressing about things but they are still getting done. I have time to listen to my family, and also for me, but I am also feeling fulfilled with work. I enjoy the time I devote to it, and it makes me feel energised, not emotionally drained. It's the emotional aspect that is key for me. I am very organised and I can cope with being physically tired through being busy, but I really struggle when I am emotionally overloaded, so that's my litmus test!

"It is absolutely possible to be both a mum and a successful business owner – you just have to OWN it!"

Erin Thomas Wong

How does your work/life balance look?

Right now, probably still not quite right. My portfolio of work isn't quite working with the right balance, and that is having a stressful knock-on effect, but overall it is a million times better than when I was employed and than when I started out.

What does a typical work day look like for you?

The structure of a 'typical' day can depend on which 'strand' of work I'm focusing on (my associate consultancy work, my coaching business or my jewellery) as to exactly how things work. But, generally my working day will start after my son and husband have left for school and work, and I usually try to grab half an hour to just clear my head and the kitchen before I then focus on work. Mornings are my most productive time, so I get my head down as close to 9am as I can and I schedule my thinking/problem solving/creative work for this time – so this is when I will write blogs, workshop content, or do some research. It's also a good time for coaching contact as I am at my best in terms of listening well! I usually break for lunch at around one – and I'm quite strict with myself about this to make sure I get up and move around!

In the afternoon I have a couple of hours before my son arrives home from school, and this is the time when I try to schedule more admin based things, or catch-up/networking calls. I do try to ensure that I am not working much beyond 4pm, when my son gets home, and I try to keep at least one day during the week completely work-free.

I also am quite disciplined about the things that I do for

I have worked to tackle personal blocks to moving forward, and found ways to help me take action when I'm scared!!

my health and wellbeing, which includes making sure I get outside every day, for at least 10 to 15 mins, ideally longer! I do sometimes feel guilty, and that I 'should' be working more, but I feel that it's important to make sure you take breaks, and that you get active – it's very easy when you work from home to stay there and not move all day!!

How important has it been to have the right support and what impact has having that support had on your business and success?

Vital. I think it's possible to source support from many different places but, however you do it, you do need to find and access that help. I have sought support for practical business issues, like knowing how to look at a marketing plan, how to think about and find your niche, using social media, doing accounts for tax returns and so on, and also for talking through ideas. I have also looked to other experts to take on some of the technical stuff around websites that I just can't face learning about. And I have worked to tackle personal blocks to moving forward, and found ways to help me take action when I'm scared!!

If you had your time again, is there anything you would do differently?

Yes. I would worry less about having posh business cards, logos and other such artefacts early on, as I managed without them for quite a while. Actually, you can do an awful lot for free or very low cost until you have settled into what you are doing. That will evolve, and quite quickly sometimes!

I would also spend less time listening to people telling me what they think I should do, and more time listening to my own whisper. I would have avoided some wrong turns had I done that!

What's next for you?

Tweaking the balance of my portfolio by evolving my jewellery business by getting to more fairs, linking up with other local craftspeople as part of a community, and setting up an online shop. I also plan to develop the coaching side of my work, which is where I really want to be spending more time, including integrating more nature-based elements into it. I want to pare back the proportion of time I spend on my Associate Consultancy work.

Nicole's Top Tips:

1. Listen to your Whisper – believe in yourself.

2. Start with your values – they will help guide any decisions you make and ensure that they will be the right ones for you.

3. Connect with others – however that works for you.

Key Takeaway

_____

_____

_____

_____

_____

_____

_____

_____

_____

_____

JILL PRYOR

Business Name: Blossom Lane
Creatives
Website: www.blossomlanecreatives.co.uk

Jill is Co-Director of Blossom Lane Creatives which offers Branding, Design and PR Support for women in business, helping them to clarify their brand from the roots up so they can confidently create effective messaging and marketing materials which connect with their audience and inspire them to achieve success on their own terms.

What did you do for a living before having children?

I ran the marketing and design department at docrafts, a craft distributor for outlets such as Hobbycraft and The Range. My role was really creative and varied from dreaming up new visual brand identities and designing craft products to e-marketing, web design, marketing collateral, managing a growing team of creatives and even guesting on QVC. I loved my job; it was constantly challenging, absorbing and enabled me to learn and develop my design, teaching and organisational skills.

Why did you decide to have a career change after becoming a mum?

I went back to work on a part-time basis after having my first daughter as I wanted a compromise between bringing in an income and spending time with her but, as to be expected, my job description became very limited due to my restrictive hours.

As the years went on, I began to feel more and more frustrated and gradually lost all confidence in my creative abilities. I used to be able to stand in front of a room full of people and teach but got to a point where I struggled to speak up in a meeting.

A change in management and some personal issues brought things to a head and I decided a fresh start was needed so I could work flexibly around my growing family and find my creativity again.

Did you struggle to make the transition to business owner?

The transition from being an employee to self-employed was so, so hard. My decision to leave my job was pretty impulsive so I'd had no time to plan what I was going to do. I'm a natural organiser and control freak and it felt like I was tumbleweed at the beginning with no clear direction, which didn't help. I wasn't sure what I wanted to do other than stay within the creative spectrum and make money to pay the bills.

My self-doubt was huge. At the time, I'd just lost my dad to cancer, was struggling with undiagnosed early menopause (which made me feel like I was losing my mind), and my youngest daughter's anxiety and OCD was at a peak. It was a dark time and I was a mess.

The fear of failure was huge. I felt everyone else in the freelance world had it nailed, knew what they were doing and were judging me (realistically, they would have been too busy to give me a second thought but that was my mindset at the time!). The mountain at that point seemed too huge to climb,

"The fear of failure was huge. I felt everyone else in the freelance world had it nailed, knew what they were doing and were judging me "

but I knew I had to pull it together somehow as the thought of going back into employment was not appealing.

Was there a lightbulb moment or a turning point where it all "clicked" for you?

I gradually started to find my feet working as a freelance graphic designer and very slowly began to rebuild my confidence as positive feedback from clients came through.

I found myself beginning to organically share clients with ex-colleague and PR freelancer, Emma Collins, and her positivity and drive really helped me pick myself up and focus. Having someone to talk through problems and ideas with was invaluable and we supported each other as we each developed our businesses.

The turning point for me was when we decided to combine our skill sets and set up Blossom Lane Creatives. Emma gave me the clarity, vision and mental support I needed and encouraged me to step out of my comfort zone on many occasions! I began to learn and hone my knowledge through attending workshops, events and online courses and started to feel more in control and more like the professional person I knew I used to be. In 2019 we ran a Brand & PR Workshop in collaboration with Erin and The Mumpreneur Collective. This was the first time I'd stood up and taught in over 15 years and it felt amazing!

What does success look like to you?

Success for me is getting positive feedback from clients, by making a difference to them and sharing what I've learnt on my journey. Success is being able to be creative and absorb myself completely in a project. Success is having enough money in the bank to pay my bills and treat my kids. Success is feeling at ease with myself and knowing I am doing the best I can. Success is being able to balance work and be there for my girls.

How does your work/life balance look?

Being self-employed means that some months I have a lovely work/life balance, with just enough work to keep me busy within school hours but that does go hand in hand with worrying about money!

Other months I'm juggling work, kids, house and end up working on weekends and evenings, which I don't like as it takes me away from my girls. These are the times when I have to be careful as self-care tends to be last on the priority list and things can go pear-shaped.

Over the past few years, I've realised where my cut-off line is and am trying to learn to say "Sorry, NO!" if I feel I'm on the edge of what I can cope with. I've recognised I need to be in the right mental state to keep myself sane and those around me happy and this is an on-going challenge for me, especially if a perfect job brief lands in my inbox!

Money certainly doesn't buy happiness but it does pay the bills and gives me the security I need. I was lucky to have a savings buffer when I went freelance which helped sub my income for the first few years. I need to make a certain amount each month to pay my contribution to household bills so there has been pressure to make it! The past few months have been the first time in four years that I've made more than I did prior to going freelance and I've realised how much better I feel because of it. However, I'm maxed out on the hours I can physically do so the next challenge is to make passive income alongside so I can reach the financial dream and enable my husband to make the transition to self-employment too.

"Learning for me has been key, whether it's online, face-to-face or at events. I try to learn new things to expand my knowledge all the time."

What does a typical work day look like for you?

5.45 am: An average day for me is to get up at 5.45am and spend an hour catching up on household paperwork or chores before digging the kids out of bed and doing the school run at 8.15am. I also try to use this quiet time to clear any notifications on my phone – I hate seeing them build up – and do a little social media engagement. If I'm feeling in the zone, I'll create a social media post but more often than not, time runs out!

8.30am: After the kids are dropped off, I walk the dog in the countryside regardless of the weather. I use this time to try and empty my head of any noise and then focus on what I need to achieve during the day and in what order. I can often be working on several design jobs at one time, all in different stages, so I need to be organised so I can make the most of the time before school pickup. Teddy (the dog!) has actually been a bit of a life saver for me in this respect as I've never naturally been a morning exerciser so would probably be inclined to miss this walk out if he wasn't with us and it really helps set me up for the day.

9.30am: After the walk, I stick Ted in the shower, try to stop him shaking all over my office and throw a load of washing on before starting work. I love the peace and quiet of working from home – my office gets the morning sun and I've added a mix of green plants to help me feel calm. If I have a client meeting, I try to arrange them for around 10-11am. I normally work straight through till 3pm, sometimes broken with a client call, coffee break or emptying the washing machine. My business partner, Emma, tries to work from mine at least once a week when we focus on our business, rather than being in it.

2.30-3pm: Off out for a country walk again. When I'm engrossed in a project, it can be difficult to break away but it works for me on two counts. One, if I've been stuck on a design or problem, the walk gives me perspective and I'll often have a moment of clarity when I'm out and end up creating a series of voice memos for later, and two, it gives me a chance to switch from work mode to mum mode before the school run .

3.45-4.30: Pick up the kids depending on after school clubs then home to the chaos of dinner, lunchboxes and other after school chores. This process seems to go on till around 7pm – I'm never too sure quite how this happens?!

7pm: If I've got a tight deadline, I'll often need to work between 7-9pm. Luckily, my girls are old enough to sort themselves out for bed (they just need a nudge every now and then!). My hubby is normally home by now to pick up any slack. If I'm on top of work, I'll try to go for a jog with the girls.

9pm: I try to keep this as my cut off time. I've learned from past experience that if I work after 9pm, my brain won't switch off and if I don't sleep, I'm not a happy person!

How important has it been to have the right support and what impact has having that support had on your business and success?

Without support I would have, without question, bailed from the freelance journey. Emma has been my professional rock, constantly pushing and inspiring me. Going to events with other women in the same situation has also been valuable; whilst daunting at first (I'm naturally a loner!), realising that you're not alone is a huge help.

The Cocoon and its community have been amazing too; the team offer so much support and the mumpreneur community are always on hand to answer questions or provide advice and ideas.

Learning for me has been key, whether it's online, face-to-face or at events. I try to learn new things to expand my

"Without support I would have, without question, bailed from the freelance journey."

knowledge all the time. I had a series of Skype sessions with an amazing NLP Empowerment Coach who helped boost my confidence and learn about the benefits of mindfulness and how to find it.

If you had your time again, is there anything you would do differently?

With hindsight, I would have planned my exit from work in advance and given myself time to come up with a plan. I'd have sorted my portfolio, done my research and felt organised and prepared so I could start my journey with a head start! The other key thing I would do differently is brand building. My experience prior to freelancing was in visual brand identity but my journey since has shown me that building a brand is not just about a logo, colour or typeface. It's so much more than that. If you spend the time and effort on building strong brand foundations then everything else falls into place naturally; from knowing what content to create on your social platforms to how to word a landing page or email.

A properly-built brand will save you a ton of headaches, stress and brain block. It will save you from the cost and effort of having to rebrand your visual identity when you realise down the line that you got it wrong.

We made these mistakes, and that's with our background! I wish we'd known at the beginning what we do now, but we've learnt and understand how great brand foundations are the key to creative effective design, marketing collateral and PR.

What's next for you?

The more I've worked with female entrepreneurs, the more I realise how many of them struggle with their branding, just like we did. Not necessarily their visual identity but the fundamental foundations which prop up their brands and help them drive it forward. If you've done the groundwork, it makes marketing your product or service so much easier.

We also know that if you have a framework to follow, it makes the process of brand building and PR so much easier. There's so much conflicting information on branding on the internet it can blow your mind, so we've used all our experience and new-found knowledge to create the 'Brand Recipe' framework which we will be using in 2020 as the basis for our coaching and online course.

Jill's Top Tips:

1. Work on your brand foundations before you create your visual identity, it makes everything else so much easier!

2. Remember that nobody is judging you, it's all in your head. The only people that care about what you do are your friends, family and colleagues. No-one else matters.

3. Be realistic about what you can achieve in the time you have available. Give yourself two or three small goals weekly which you know you can achieve in order to keep you motivated and your business moving forward.

Key Takeaway

MELANIE MOSS

Business name: Melanie Moss
Photography
Website: www.melaniemoss.com

Melanie is a freelance photographer living in London. She loves working with all types of businesses and people. Much of her work is focused on headshots and family portraits but she also works with schools, events and dance. She is married with two teenage children and is passionate about running, skiing, and coffee.

What did you do for a living before having children?
Before I had children I worked for the British Red Cross Society. Whilst doing Geography at university I had realised that I wanted to work for an organisation that helped communities at home and overseas. I had a gap year teaching in India and Nepal, then travelled around Asia before doing a Masters in International Development. My first proper job was working for an international logistics organisation, moving relief goods into Kosovo during the Bosnia-Herzegovina war. This helped me get my dream job at the British Red Cross working on international development projects. I loved the whole environment in the charity sector as it was all centred around working with others to help them build and strengthen their own communities. People were ambitious and driven but compassionate and caring towards each other, and I absolutely loved my job, but I realise now that what I loved most of all was understanding what makes people tick and helping them to support others.

Why did you decide to have a career change after becoming a mum?

Going back to the Red Cross part-time after having each of my two children was great to start with and definitely gave me the confidence to get my work-head back. But, soon after returning the second time, it became clear that my job would change quite radically and if I wanted to continue being project-focused I would have to travel more regularly than I had been and be more flexible. This suddenly tipped the balance of job satisfaction, work-life balance and pay. Getting a nanny so I could reposition myself would have netted out paying to go to work, and I realised that what I wanted was to have more hours with my children, not less. My years of employment had given me a whole range of technical, finance, admin, and comms skills, and I had been secretly harbouring an ambition to see if I could apply them to running a project of my own. Also at that time, I was learning to use a digital camera and really enjoying it.

One weekend, I was spending time with old school friends and telling them about my conundrum of what to do with my job and family/work balance when suddenly it all made sense. I realised that I had to jump into the void of no longer being employed and see how it felt. I had a quick text chat with my husband about my conclusions and by the time the train arrived back at Paddington Station I had already decided to resign on Monday morning.

"...suddenly it all made sense. I realised that I had to jump into the void of no longer being employed and see how it felt"

Did you struggle to make the transition to business owner?

The helpful thing about working for a charity and paying two lots of childcare was that I wasn't used to making a lot of profit from going to work. Fortunately, both children were old enough to have state nursery or playgroup time so I did have a few hours of free childcare which helped me take six months to start researching and preparing to set up a photography business as well as do some in-depth training courses. With photography, you have the option of setting up relatively slowly without having to dive in with a big start up investment cost. For me, this was the best business model to take as it all felt quite low risk, and I was not under pressure to earn a full wage immediately.

Everything was ready to go apart from my head. Imposter syndrome was the only thing holding me back, but it was quite huge. How on earth do you suddenly start calling yourself a photography business owner when a year ago you were working in a totally different setting? Thankfully I have a hugely supportive husband and some great friends who didn't question what I was doing and pushed me forward for jobs that came near my path. I might still be waiting for the imposter syndrome cloud to shift otherwise ;)

A photographer friend told me that the first few years are the hardest and it really helped me to know this. There will always be ups and downs in running any business, but the initial challenge of setting one up is like wading through porridge. Every problem seemed to have a host of other issues attached to it that needed solving before things could progress: so one step forward, three steps back. I am a real completer-finisher and I place a lot of value on detail. This is very helpful for preparing and briefing for jobs and great for customer service but hugely frustrating when problems can't be solved quickly and there's only one of you to do it, so at the beginning there was a lot of shouting at my Mac in my office and going for a run in the park.

The hardest thing that I find now, 11 years in, is when I am overly desk-based. Often in months which are packed with photoshoots I have very limited time to do business development and marketing work, so these are the jobs that I feel I have to concentrate on in quieter times. I'm a very self-motivated person but gain energy from being around and interacting with people, so it presses all my self-belief and morale buttons when I'm just sat at my desk. It's taken me long enough but over the years I've realised that I just have to get out of my office and work remotely when I feel like this. The morning chat, banter and coffee that I used to have for ten minutes with my colleagues before we all got started on our work each day has to be replaced by a quick cycle to my local coffee house, without feeling decadent or guilty about it.

Was there a lightbulb moment or a turning point where it all "clicked" for you?

I can't say that I've ever experienced a lightbulb moment in setting up and running my business with confidence, more a gradual brightening-up of the dimmer switch. I am what you would term a generalist photographer and for a while I had a bit of a problem and insecurity about the fact that most (but definitely not all) photographers specialise in, say, baby and family photography, or weddings, products, headshots. I always compared my brand and marketing to the various specialists and then felt inadequate. And I certainly don't enjoy talking about the really technical side of photography. Don't get me

"The realisation that I can make my business work on my own terms and based on my own strengths, rather than comparing myself to others, has been really liberating."

wrong, I've done plenty of technical courses and feel more than equipped with technical ability but I am very intuitive in my approach to jobs and I've got a rubbish memory for things that I don't need to remember so please never quiz me on the names of battery packs! I've never wanted to specialise as I love the variety and challenge of working with different people and different types and sizes of organisations.

The thing that has helped me suddenly become more at ease with the service that I offer is that I've realised the common theme of my service is the ability to work well with people and engage with them so that they very quickly feel comfortable with me and with being in front of the camera. This is obviously essential for capturing the expressions and emotions that they need for themselves or their businesses. I just have to accept the reality of marketing to different types of people, including looking to different social media platforms for different audiences, and realise that this takes a bit more time to master and won't appear as perfectly polished as a specialist's marketing.

What does success look like to you?

The realisation that I can make my business work on my own terms and based on my own strengths, rather than comparing myself to others, has been really liberating. For any business to develop and grow it is critical that you know what your unique selling point is and if you set up from scratch I think it takes time to properly understand this. I'm happy now that I know what my added value is and how I can build on my business with this. And this feels like success.

How does your work/life balance look?

When my children were younger but at school, I was able to give them plenty of hands-on time and facilitate their busy clubs and social lives which felt good while running a business. It was exhausting nevertheless as, although my hours were often flexible, it simply meant I stopped work at 3pm and retreated to my desk at 8 or 9pm once they were in bed and I'd had something to eat. Working until 3am was a fairly common occurrence in busy photoshoot weeks. That's when the cycle and coffee routine was even more crucial.

At times you feel exhausted and at a loss that you're doing anything as well as you want to but most of the time the flexibility brings huge benefits. I used to often feel guilty about how I was dividing my time between work and children, and to an extent that would be a feature whichever job I do, but the best thing I did when the children were really little was to stop using a laptop and stick to a desktop as it prevented work-creep into the kitchen or where the children played. As the children became teenagers and much more independent the work-life balance has felt much better and I've been able to be around to chat to them (obviously only when they want to!) without so much ferrying them about which eroded a good deal of potential work time.

A very wise Red Cross colleague who had much older children once said to me "You can't choose when teenagers want to talk to you so you just have to put in the hours to be there". I really feel that running my own business helped me put the hours in. The really lovely part is that now they've mostly come out of the terrible teenage years they seem to appreciate that I've built a business and sometimes I can even bribe them to pack my orders!

What does a typical work day look like for you?

Most days are pretty different as some will be early starts with day-long photoshoots and others with shorter photoshoots interspersing the day, or editing and working at my desk for the full day. Now that my children are 16 and 18 I no longer have the school run juggle but I still try to be around in the morning before school for a quick chat if I can, and then cycle to a coffee shop to set me up and get my head in gear for whatever

"...Mentoring was really key as it not only helped develop my existing skills in the business-related areas but supported the belief in myself that I could do it. "

is planned. Usually I'm at my desk or setting up for a shoot by 9.30am latest. Where feasible I try to do client meetings and photoshoots before 4 or 5pm so that I'm back working at home with an open door policy.

On a quieter day if I'm lucky I might even get to sneak off to the gym with my daughter when she's back from school. The washing gets done in and around the day whenever I can or whenever it's overflowed, but everything else has to wait until the evening – though at least then it's more visible and my husband gets to share it :)

How important has it been to have the right support and what impact has having that support had on your business and success?

Working out what sort of support and training you might need in setting up and running a business is vital. I knew that I wanted to have some more technical training and did a number of high quality photography and software courses part-time in the first five years and then various top-ups since then. A few very good friends who were all specialists in their work areas were amazingly helpful and became unofficial mentors and sounding-boards when I first set up. It was fantastic, I appeared to have the full complement of Creative, IT, Commercial, Finance, and Marketing mentors covered which helped me massively in terms of support but also in identifying where my gaps of knowledge lay initially.

In hindsight, if I'd not had these brilliant unofficial mentors

I definitely should have budgeted to pay one or more people to mentor in some of these areas. Mentoring was really key as it not only helped develop my existing skills in the business-related areas but supported the belief in myself that I could do it. And when you have other people talking to you like you run a professional business you start to overcome the imposter chimp in your head and really begin to believe that maybe you are? All along the way I've benefited hugely from going to various network groups too. I've attended the whole spectrum of types, from very structured monthly paid groups to informal coffee business chat groups. All have had their merits and been valuable in different ways and according to my changing needs. The Cocoon has been fantastic as a constant networking group for the past three years. It's more of a community than just a network and one offering tonnes of support in a flexibly-timed way. It feels like I have someone just looking out for me and my business (as well as challenging me) but without the pressures of having to attend at specific times – something that is impossible when my photoshoots and client meetings can be different days and times each week. It's been a brilliant way of connecting to a cacophony of businesses and the Momentum Days have then added to my hands-on business training as well as putting names to faces that I've got to know online.

If you had your time again, is there anything you would do differently?

If I was setting up business all over again from now, the main thing I would try and change is the length of time that it's taken me to feel unapologetic about charging proper prices. Clearly at the beginning you don't want to be turning away too many jobs but I would advise my earlier business self to be happy with charging a reasonable price for the time and skill involved and accept that it will shed a few potential customers but they are therefore not my target audience.

In real terms, I'm probably earning about the same as I was

in a permanent job. It's obviously less secure, and comes with a worry at times because of that, but the plus side is that it's within my control to grow my business and my income.

What's next for you?

I love my business and am really proud of what I have set up. But I love even more the opportunities that it provides to engage with a multitude of people and the businesses that I encounter and learn about. I see learning, regularly putting ourselves out of our comfort zones and interacting with different people as three key elements in a happy life, at all ages. I want to keep growing my business but my aim is to ensure that these three factors will continue to feature.

Melanie's Top Tips:

1. Surround yourself with people who you trust and will challenge you but also support you. Don't listen to naysayers.

2. If you possibly can, keep startup costs low. Some businesses are easier than others for this however.

3. Consider which factors in your previous work environment you will miss most and try to find ways of plugging these gaps.

Key Takeaway

_____

_____

_____

_____

_____

_____

_____

_____

KAREN MERRYWEATHER

Business Name: Little Pickle Deli Cafe
Website: www.littlepickledelicafe.co.uk

Karen's career started in customer services, holiday repping in the sunny isles of Greece in her twenties. After taking a year off to travel around Australia, the fabulous cafes of Melbourne had an impact on her, and her lifelong dream became to open a business with the same feel as an Australian street cafe. Karen and her New Zealand-born husband Andrew now own and run a busy family-friendly cafe in Bournemouth, serving locally sourced, great quality food to the local community.

What did you do for a living before having children?
I spent a lot of my career in the holiday industry. I worked for First Choice for five years before joining British Airways as ground staff for Concorde and First Class passengers. I then changed industries and spent ten years working as a Financial Analyst for a software company before having my two girls.

Why did you decide to have a career change after becoming a mum?
I wanted the flexibility of being my own boss, in charge of my own time, and to be there for our girls when it came to school trips, performances or just running them to and from dance classes or gymnastics. It was important to us as we had no family support to help us, having moved down from Reading. We also wanted to be able to enjoy the beach and an

impromptu BBQ, so if school's out and the sun is shining that is where you will find us.

Did you struggle to make the transition to business owner?

We experienced a lot of doubt from other people when it came to opening Little Pickle. Nobody expected it to work in the area we set up in because it was different to what was already there. But we lived in the area and we knew that people there wanted to see a cafe like ours open locally. We could not get finance for the cafe so we built it from scratch. We recycled furniture from second hand shops, bought crockery from car boot stalls and roped in friends to help renovate the premises. Initially, I had help with child-care as I had just given birth to my second daughter when the cafe opened its doors for the first time. I was combining breastfeeding a newborn with running a cafe, which was rather overwhelming, so we employed a nanny who had barista skills too, so that she and I could swap roles when necessary! She was integral in helping me retain my sanity during this period of madness.

Was there a lightbulb moment or a turning point where it all "clicked" for you?

I am not sure if there has ever been a lightbulb moment, but the pleasure of people enjoying the cafe has never left me. We opened Little Pickle in 2012 and I still love seeing happy customers enjoying good food in surroundings they love. It's shabby chic meets seaside vintage and it just works.

What does success look like to you?

Success is seeing the cafe busy and buzzing, regulars using it on a daily basis and being able to host events that bring people together. It's managing a team that are loyal, long standing, and happy to be providing the sort of service you love. It's a family business and we like people to feel that they are part of ours. I think success for cafés these days is just surviving the ups and downs, it's a bit of a roller coaster but we are holding on and enjoying the ride.

How does your work/life balance look?

Work/life balance is always a challenge and something that needs to be worked at. I am not great at taking time off as there is always something to do in the cafe or at home. 2020 is definitely my year to get the balance back and for that I am joining a local choir and learning to dance cha-cha-cha! I do yoga and meditation when I am feeling things getting on top of me as I find both of them very calming. They give me space in my head to think more clearly.

What does a typical work day look like for you?

My typical day starts with getting our girls ready for school. I normally do this as my husband starts work every morning at 8am. I then do the house chores, tidy up and put a load of washing on before I check my emails for the day, I follow up quotes, enquiries and do general admin for the café. At lunchtime I head into the café to give a hand if necessary or sometimes have a meeting with a customer regarding an event. It can be manic some days so back up is well received. I pick up the girls at 3.15pm and ferry them back and forth to clubs. Not every day is the same, some days we have outside catering on, so I manage that. Every day is different, the weeks move fast, it can feel a bit crazy at times but that's how we roll..

How important has it been to have the right support and what impact has having that support had on your business and success?

It's massively important to find the right support, and to invest time and money in yourself and in your business. I feel most inspired when I have moved out of my comfort zone and taken part in networking events or attended one of Erin's amazing

Momentum days. They make you feel like you can achieve all your dreams, that anything is possible and that you are doing so much right already. The Cocoon has been a great way to meet some amazing women, share advice, ask questions in confidence without fear and feel like you are part of a wonderful, strong, knowledgeable, and supportive community.

If you had your time again, is there anything you would do differently?

I believe everything happens for a reason so, no, I would not do anything differently.

What's next for you?

This year we are looking to get an alcohol licence, to hold more private parties and expand our catering services. We are great at doing events but need to market ourselves to a wider audience. The cafe is the perfect spot for a party, a gig, a talk or a craft night so it's just a case of finding the right people to make these events possible.

"I believe everything happens for a reason so no I would not do anything differently."

Karen's Top Tips:

1. Create a business you are passionate about.

2. Find the right people to support you.

3. Take a day off when you need it.

Key Takeaway

_____

_____

_____

_____

_____

_____

_____

_____

_____

_____

_____

_____

_____

MARION ELLIS
FRICS CCXP

Business Name: BlueBox Partners
Website: www.blueboxpartners.com

Marion is a residential chartered surveyor and valuer with a specialised background in complaints and claims. She is managing director of BlueBox Partners – an alliance of experienced valuers and surveyors committed to supporting the professional development, and personal well-being of others in the industry. Marion is also a qualified women's leadership coach and customer experience specialist.

What did you do for a living before having children?
I have been working in the residential property sector for over 20 years and, prior to having children, was a residential surveyor and valuer carrying out mortgage valuations and home surveys. Before I trained, I did every admin job under the sun and worked in many customer service and call centre roles.

Why did you decide to have a career change after becoming a mum?
It didn't happen for me immediately and it certainly wasn't planned, I wasn't brave enough back then to even dream of working for myself – what would I do? After I had my daughter I had a challenging return to work after maternity leave and although I stuck at it for three years I realised I had got to a point in my life and career where I wasn't prepared to put up with living in fear of my boss, frustrated that I wasn't making a difference in the things that mattered and my health and mental health was suffering.

Did you struggle to make the transition to business owner?

At first, I set up my own business delivering consultancy training for construction firms in customer experience and ethics. I enjoyed some of it but it didn't float my boat. When I left my Board level corporate role, I really didn't think anyone would employ me, so I never thought to apply for a job and that is how I initially ended up working for myself. I have done quite a bit of personal development over the past few years and so stepping away without a job or career to go to was the calmest yet scariest thing I have ever done. I just had to trust that I would be ok. There is so much to learn about setting up by yourself, at times it is exciting and other times it is unbelievably overwhelming, non-stop learning.

Was there a lightbulb moment or a turning point where it all "clicked" for you?

Setting up on my own was a massive learning curve. I learned though, that I hate being by myself and yet at the opposite range of the spectrum I didn't want to be employed anymore. Things clicked into place when I was asked to lead BlueBox Partners where I am part owner and managing director. It was a great opportunity to have just enough support to make me feel secure and enough freedom to allow my creative skills to flourish.

What does success look like to you?

Success for me was always about money. It is hard for it not to be, as money changes so much and creates freedom to pursue the things that matter to you. A stable income that allows me to pay for the family holiday and some savings is enough now though. Interestingly when I left my corporate job, I stopped emotional spending like clothes shopping in order to escape and to feel I always looked the part. It was quite an eye-opener and brought a real sense of relief.

I have just been appointed to the Royal Institution of

Chartered Surveyors (RICS) Global Governing Council which is a huge step-up in experience for me. I would never have been brave enough in the past, so to be in a position where I can influence change in the world feels like success even if it is a volunteer non-executive role.

How does your work/life balance look?

It fluctuates. I have periods of having to be away, and the stress over childcare can create a real mental load, but mostly I am now around for school pick-up. I find it hard though when I make the effort to stop work to collect the children from school and they don't want to know me, or they argue. Rhythm and routine seem to be the key to it with the children. I also know that I am too busy, so a focus for me in the coming year is to not do so much of the free volunteer stuff and be selective.

I often talk about work-life integration with my clients rather than balance. It is hard to be different people doing different things; it takes a lot of energy. Now I try to bring me – a working mum and a mum who works – to everything I do and it feels much more comfortable and authentic.

How important has it been to have the right support and what impact has having that support had on your business and success?

When I walked away from my corporate job, I thought I had no network and no support. They were dark days. What I did was give myself time, stopped feeling like a victim, and

Through my personal development networks, I met so many women who did everything from creating pictures from buttons on their kitchen table to running huge successful PR firms.

shared my experience with my professional network. They helped me enormously and gave me strength. Through my personal development networks, I met so many women who did everything from creating pictures from buttons on their kitchen table to running huge successful PR firms. Now that I was working for myself I just had to ask and I would get recommendations, hints and tips. I had to find my way and explore how I wanted to make money in the future. That took time, and it is still evolving, but the support I have had is incredible. You just don't see the same combination of business and wellbeing support in such an open and friendly way in corporate environments.

If you had your time again, is there anything you would do differently?

I would learn all about how to set up a business, I was beyond naive. I was recommended an accountant who was awful and I was too scared to ask her a question. I would learn more about websites because I had a run-in with a developer. It is easy to be taken advantage of when you have a passion and excitement for your idea and want to just crack on. I would also read the book 'Profit First' by Mike Michalowicz, which has been a game-changer for my business.

What's next for you?

I am growing The Surveyor Hub community and I am launching some online group coaching programmes, memberships and subscription services but mainly continuing to learn and grow. Once I accepted that being a small business is a constant learning journey it felt like a weight had lifted. Now I feel free to experiment and see what works and what doesn't.

Marion's Top Tips:

1. Get good small business advice.

2. Keep a list of books and professionals recommended to you.

3. Find an accountant you can really talk to.

Key Takeaway

_____

_____

_____

_____

_____

_____

_____

_____

_____

_____

_____

_____

ERIN THOMAS WONG

Business Name:
The Mumpreneur Collective
Website: www.mumpreneurcollective.com

Erin is a mentor, speaker, champion of
mums in business and founder of
The Mumpreneur Collective and The Cocoon online
business club. She has built five businesses over the
last 12 years whilst raising two very active little boys!

What did you do for a living before having children?

Before my first son I had a successful career in TV Production
working in London on some fantastic programmes like the
MTV Awards, Scrapheap Challenge and Celebrity Wifeswap.
Since the age of about 14 I had done loads of free work
experience, getting up at 5am to help on a morning radio
show, and travelling by train for an hour to work on a local TV
programme. I was completely focused on getting that first paid
job, and once I graduated from university I secured a position
at the BBC within months. Over the next eight years I worked
my way up from a Runner to a Production Manager.

Why did you decide to have a career change after becoming a mum?

I loved being in a team and the fast-paced schedule was a buzz,
but I started to realise it would be difficult to balance that kind
of career with having a family.

When I fell pregnant I made the plan to take a year off on
maternity leave to gaze into my baby's eyes and be the earth
mother I always felt I would be… Boy was I in for a shock!

After a traumatic emergency c-section, my milk not coming

in, and the most horrendous sleep deprivation, being a new parent was not what I had envisaged!! Within a few months I realised that I was losing myself and I needed to get some control back.

I just couldn't imagine going back to my career in TV, with the often late nights in the office and emergency calls on the weekends. And financially it seemed ridiculous that, after the cost of childcare, I would be working full-time and only end up with a few hundred pounds in my pocket a month, and that was on a good salary!

Then the universe called. I found out about a fingerprint jewellery company called Smallprint, which offered a franchise where they taught you to make and sell bespoke silver keepsakes that capture fingerprints, hand and footprints. I had never considered running my own business before but suddenly this became a very real and exciting option.

Some of my friends and family had doubts. They were concerned I would feel lonely going from working in a lively team to working alone. All I can say is that it felt like the most liberating and compelling opportunity, and it felt absolutely right.

I was fortunate to qualify for voluntary redundancy, so I used that money to invest in this new business venture.

So there I was, taking my first steps into the world of small business. My baby was now six months old and life was beginning to normalise. At last, there was space in my head to think beyond the next nappy change.

Did you struggle to make the transition to business owner?

Taking on a franchise was a sharp learning curve, but becoming my own boss was the most empowering experience, and it felt like I regained some of the control that I felt I had lost during childbirth and the early months.

I really enjoyed running Smallprint, and it gave me the confidence to develop other business ideas which quickly came to fruition – Ealing Mums in Business (events & networking meetups) and Pitter Patter – The Hub For Bubs (venues for baby & toddler classes) and later, The Kids' Nature Shop (an online shop encouraging children to play outdoors).

But don't get me wrong – sometimes I was riddled with self-doubt, I questioned my decisions on a daily basis and held myself back due to fear of failure. I was also really nervous about speaking in front of people, and for a long time hid behind my business partner, Shelley Henderson, when we held meetups for Ealing Mums in Business. She kept encouraging me to speak, but it felt so uncomfortable that it was easier to let her do it than to face my fears.

For me, what helped was meeting other women in business and taking comfort in the fact that I wasn't alone in these feelings. This was one of the very first lessons I learned as an entrepreneur – together we're stronger, so find those people that you can confide in and let them support you.

My proudest moment was being recognised by our local MP for our work as Ealing Mums in Business with a reception in the Houses of Parliament. The evening was one of the most amazing experiences of my life.

Was there a lightbulb moment or a turning point where it all "clicked" for you?

In 2015 the opportunity arose for my family to move to Abu Dhabi for my husband's job. This experience was life-changing in many ways.

It gave me a much clearer focus on how I wanted to live my

"...together we're stronger, so find those people that you can confide in and let them support you."

"*Do one thing every day to stay visible*"

Erin Thomas Wong

life, and the kind of business I wanted to run. It needed to be online to give me flexibility. I wanted to carry on working with mums in business, but I wanted to do it on a wider scale. Being 7,000 miles away from everyone I knew felt very isolating and my first lightbulb moment was the realisation that there are women all over the world setting up businesses, with no support network at all. I wanted to fill that gap.

This is when The Mumpreneur Collective (formerly Making Mumpreneurs) was born. The Mumpreneur Collective is an online community which supports and empowers mums around the world running their businesses around family life, through support, tips and inspiration. No matter where you are in your business journey, I've got the resources to help.

Just as the business was launching, we had to make a difficult decision. Life in Abu Dhabi didn't suit us, and my husband and I were becoming increasingly unhappy. It was at this point that we decided to call it quits, and move back to the UK, this time to Bournemouth on the South Coast, to live by sea and create a better quality of life.

This is when having launched an online business came in to its own, as we were able to pack up and move, and bring the business with us.

In Bournemouth, I immersed myself in the incredible entrepreneurial vibe and started making contacts and building

"Being 7,000 miles away from everyone I knew felt very isolating and my first lightbulb moment was the realisation that there are women all over the world setting up businesses, with no support network at all. I wanted to fill that gap.

an audience to add to the growing community I was already developing online.

The business quickly blossomed but I wanted to take it further and offer more because I knew there was a need for more accessible business training for women. So after a year I launched The Cocoon business club, a subscription membership group. It's a safe, more intimate, place to learn, evolve and grow as a small business owner. I've been able to collaborate with all the amazing business experts I've met over the last 12 years to provide hugely valuable content. The members benefit from monthly masterclasses, expert advice, accountability, camaraderie, ongoing support seven days a week, and most importantly feel part of a wider team, all from the comfort of their own home.

This is a unique proposition for those mums caring for children at home who may not be able to get out to networking events. It can be incredibly lonely and isolating being a mum sometimes, and, if you throw in running a business from home into the mix, it can be a real challenge. But it's so important to have the right support around you, not only teaching you new skills as you grow, but also inspiring and motivating you on a daily basis.

I've grown in confidence tremendously over the last few years. I realised very quickly that when it comes to public speaking, if I wasn't prepared to do it for The Mumpreneur Collective, no one else would do it for me, and I wouldn't reach the people I wanted to. So I invested in help, got over my fear, and now I enjoy speaking to audiences, live and online, as well as hosting regular Facebook Lives and our one-day Momentum Day conference twice a year.

What does success look like to you?

For me, success means having a thriving business doing something which brings me joy every day, dictating my own hours, and earning great money so that we can enjoy the nice things in life.

Over the years my income has varied, and I have re-invested much of the profit back into the business so I can focus on the long game. I've built a scalable business which encompasses all the things I love and which is not wholly reliant on a time-for-money basis. This feels incredibly empowering.

How does your work/life balance look?

After 12 years I have this pretty nailed! Both my kids are at school now so my core working hours are 9.00–2.30pm. My business is heavily based on social media so I am of course checking messages once they are at home and in to the evening, but this is because I want to, not because I have to. I know how hard it is to get this balance right, and it's one thing I love helping others to achieve.

During school holidays I don't take calls or meetings, or run big projects. This means I can be flexible around the kids and only work if the opportunity comes up. I do often wake up naturally very early, and so I embrace that extra hour to tick some things off before the kids wake up!

How important has it been to have the right support and what impact has having that support had on your business and success?

Having a support network has been absolutely invaluable and fundamental to my success as an entrepreneur. From the early days of Ealing Mums in Business when I was able to physically surround myself with like-minded women, to now knowing all I need to do is log in to The Cocoon to chat to my tribe 24/7 has made a huge difference to my mental wellbeing and has banished the isolation that comes from working alone.

A couple of years ago I finally made the investment in a business mentor, with whom I work 1:1. That provides me with constant backup and advice on my strategy and day-to-day operations. This has undoubtedly made the biggest change to my business, and my happiness as a business owner. I feel well supported which has allowed me to push through my comfort zone on a regular basis and keep scaling up the business. I have also now invested in a fantastic online business manager and an accountant.

I understand that people get caught in a Catch-22 of not wanting to invest in a business club, mentor or coach until they are "earning enough money" to pay for it, but the truth is, the earlier you invest in the support you need, the faster you will make that money.

If you had your time again, is there anything you would do differently?

I don't like to have regrets because I think everything is a learning experience, and along the way I have learned more from when things have gone wrong than from things going right. I wish I had been kinder to myself though, and worked on my feelings of self-doubt and low confidence sooner. I definitely would have gotten to where I am now a lot faster if I had done that.

What's next for you?

The Mumpreneur Collective goes from strength to strength and I am scaling my mentoring practice, growing The Cocoon business club and introducing new in-person business events. My mission is to help mothers become happier and more successful business owners, designing a business that works for them AROUND family life. One that they jump out of bed in the morning for, and one that fills them with joy on a daily basis. It is absolutely possible to be both a mum and a successful business owner – you just have to OWN IT!

Erin's Top Tips:

1. Your business will evolve – don't be afraid of things not working out. We learn from failure not success.

2. Don't try to do everything alone – invest in the right support

3. Find your tribe who will support you when times are tough and celebrate with you when things go well.

Key Takeaway

_____

_____

_____

_____

_____

_____

_____

_____

_____

_____

CONCLUSION

In this book you've heard from women at different stages of their businesses, in completely different industries, and with children in a range of age groups, but did you notice there are many common themes?

All of them have come up against challenges and crossroads, for which they have had to dig deep, make a decision, and take action to move forward.

Many have mentioned self-doubt, or imposter syndrome. In fact, most of the women I have worked with over the last 12 years have experienced this at some point during their career. The message of this book is that it's OK to doubt yourself sometimes – after all, self-criticism can be a useful tool – but don't allow it to paralyse you. Remember, instead, that true growth always happens just outside your comfort zone.

Take note of the heart-stopping moment described by so many in these pages – the point at which they felt the fear and did it anyway!

They also talk about how empowered they feel being able to run their own business, dictate their hours, and be their own boss.

All of them are running a business successfully on their terms – they are building in flexibility around their kids, working around childcare and doing what they love to do.

But nobody said it would be easy. In 2019, the Rose Review of Female Entrepreneurship* reported that women are twice as likely as men to mention family responsibilities as a barrier to starting a business, and many cite a lack of relatable mentors as one of the issues they have to overcome...

I've been there. I get it. And I'm here to help.

This is why finding your tribe is so important. We need to support each other and rise up together.

You too can build a business you love that works around family life – it's time to spread those wings and fly!

Join us in The Mumpreneur Collective, be part of the movement and start carving your own path today.

We've got your back!

www.mumpreneurcollective.com

 @mumpreneurcollective

 @erin_thomas_wong

 @erinthomaswong

*Rose Review of Female Entrepreneurship, HM Treasury 2019

THANKS & ACKNOWLEDGEMENTS

This book wouldn't be possible without the fantastic contributions from our Cocoon business club members, and their willingness to step forward and share their stories with us. Huge thanks to Amy Hobson, Anne Millne-Riley, Bonita Elms, Carly Rose, Claire Addiscott, Cori Javid, Elizabeth Lusty, Felicity Sandford, Jill Pryor, Jo Brianti, Karen Merryweather, Katherine Whitby, Keri Squibb, Laura Robinson, Louise Gates, Maija Pykett, Marion Ellis, Melanie Moss, Nicole Gabriel, Nina Mucalov, Tanya Bunting and Zoe Keeping.

Thank you to my mum, Sue Thomas, for your unending support and encouragement with this book. Thank you for being my champion.

To my team for keeping me on track, organised and energised about this project: My business coach Cori Javid, my online business manager Carly Rose, and my book designer Briony Hartley of Goldust Design.

To my husband Dominic and my mother-in-law Penny Wong, thank you for your faith in me.

And last but surely not least, to my two amazing sons Ollie & Milo, I hope our journeys inspire you to carve your own path in life.

Ready to put what you've learned from this book into action?

Download the accompanying free Evolve Workbook which will help you to:

1. Document your key takeaways from the book so that you can keep them on hand for quick reference and inspiration

2. Get clear on your goals for the upcoming year so that you can take focused action

3. Make an effective plan for business growth so you can grow and scale

4. Keep yourself accountable so you can keep making progress

Let's get designing this business on YOUR terms!

DOWNLOAD NOW AT
www.mumpreneurcollective.com/evolve

Boost your business
Learn, evolve & grow
in The Cocoon now

We have everything you need to build a business you love around family life.

Get immediate access to:

✔ A library of video masterclasses to enhance your business skills & personal development

✔ Experts on hand who have learned the lessons so you don't have to

✔ Private supportive Facebook community of like-minded people

✔ Promotion of your business to increase brand awareness

✔ Goal-setting & accountability to keep you focused so you can stay on track

The
COCOON

"If I was speaking to someone sitting on the fence about joining The Cocoon I would say do it! Invest in yourself! It's one of the best things I have done for myself and for my business this year. I feel like because of the Cocoon I'm a year ahead of where I would have been without it!"
NINA MUCALOV

"The Cocoon has been an absolute game changer for me. I'm at the very beginning of my entrepreneurial journey but the connections I have made through The Cocoon in the last six weeks are changing my life."
ERIN LEWIS

Become a member and join the women featured in this book plus many more inside The Cocoon today at:

www.mumpreneurcollective.com/cocoon

Printed in Great Britain
by Amazon